# Beat Low Self-Esteem with CBT

# Beat Low Self-Esteem with CBT

Christine Wilding and
Stephen Palmer

For UK order enquiries: please contact Bookpoint Ltd,
130 Milton Park, Abingdon, Oxon OX14 4SB.
*Telephone:* +44 (0) 1235 827720. *Fax:* +44 (0) 1235 400454.
Lines are open 09.00–17.00, Monday to Saturday, with a 24-hour
message answering service. Details about our titles and how to
order are available at www.teachyourself.com

For USA order enquiries: please contact McGraw-Hill Customer
Services, PO Box 545, Blacklick, OH 43004-0545, USA.
*Telephone:* 1-800-722-4726. *Fax:* 1-614-755-5645.

For Canada order enquiries: please contact McGraw-Hill
Ryerson Ltd, 300 Water St, Whitby, Ontario L1N 9B6,
Canada. *Telephone:* 905 430 5000. *Fax:* 905 430 5020.

Long renowned as the authoritative source for self-guided
learning – with more than 50 million copies sold worldwide –
the *Teach Yourself* series includes over 500 titles in the fields of
languages, crafts, hobbies, business, computing and education.

British Library Cataloguing in Publication Data: a catalogue record
for this title is available from the British Library.

Library of Congress Catalog Card Number: on file.

First published in UK 2010 by Hodder Education, part of Hachette
UK, 338 Euston Road, London NW1 3BH.

First published in US 2010 by The McGraw-Hill Companies, Inc.

This edition published 2010.

Typeset by MPS Limited, a Macmillan Company.

Printed in Great Britain for Hodder Education, an Hachette UK
Company, 338 Euston Road, London NW1 3BH, by
CPI Group (UK) Ltd, Croydon, CR0 4YY.

The publisher has used its best endeavours to ensure that the URLs
for external websites referred to in this book are correct and active
at the time of going to press. However, the publisher and the author
have no responsibility for the websites and can make no guarantee
that a site will remain live or that the content will remain relevant,
decent or appropriate.

Hachette UK's policy is to use papers that are natural, renewable
and recyclable products and made from wood grown in sustainable
forests. The logging and manufacturing processes are expected to
conform to the environmental regulations of the country of origin.

Impression number       10  9  8  7  6  5  4
Year                    2014  2013  2012

# Contents

# Meet the authors

## Welcome to *Beat Low Self-Esteem with* CBT!

Enhancing self-esteem sounds easy. Start a relationship, buy and wear some new clothes, pass an exam or two at college and get promoted at work. If it's that easy, why do so many of us suffer from low self-esteem some – or all – of the time? If you do question why and want to overcome your plummeting self-esteem, this book may provide the answers and solutions you are looking for.

As a coaching and counselling psychologist (Stephen Palmer) and a psychotherapist (Christine Wilding), we work on a daily basis with people and teams who suffer from a lack of self-esteem. These people may present to us with a variety of different problems, ranging from chronic depression and anxiety to seeing their lives fall apart after a job loss, close bereavement, relationship breakdown or other serious life events. But one of the common threads running through this wide variety of problems is that these people are unable to deal successfully with these issues without professional help because life events trigger a reduction in self-esteem which subsequently undermines their confidence to problem solve.

As professionally qualified practitioners, we are not actually there to resolve people's personal crises. We have no magical powers! We are there to facilitate a person's own resources to troubleshoot their problems and develop solutions, thereby tackling their self-esteem issues too. We also provide a range of low-self-esteem busting skills and techniques, based on cognitive behavioural therapies (CBT) that can be applied by you.

It is these skills and techniques that we would like to share with you in this book.

Christine Wilding and Stephen Palmer

# *Only got a minute?*

So what is self-esteem? Self-esteem can best be described as your own abilities and values. It does not mean thinking you are the best at everything, but feeling comfortable with yourself even when you are not. It is accepting yourself, with all your strengths and weaknesses, while still taking opportunities for self-development.

This suggests that if we perform well or have positive attributes, then we can feel good about ourselves and our self-esteem is raised. Self-esteem is, in essence, a measurement based on our own or others' criteria of what's good.

However, if we negatively appraise our attributes or performance, the downside is that we may lower our self-esteem and end up feeling depressed and sorry for ourselves. A typical example would be failing at an important exam and directly linking our performance with a global measurement or rating of ourselves. We may think: 'As I failed my important exam, this proves I'm a total failure as a person. What's the point of continuing with my studies?' It's no wonder we can make ourselves feel miserable at times.

The good news is that using cognitive behavioural therapy (CBT), or coaching, we can modify our thinking. In this example, after some self-coaching, we may think instead: 'I failed my important exam. It just means I'm fallible. I'll have another go later in the year.' Accepting what we have done while not 'rating' or beating ourselves up, contributes to the development of good self-esteem, better known as self-acceptance. It becomes easier to move forward and not waste much time on what's happened. This approach can be very liberating as it allows us to embrace challenges and confront the fear of failure. We are more likely to give a difficult task or project a go; we cease putting our ego on the line, and just rate our skills or skills deficits.

# 5 Only got five minutes?

As a culture, most of us accept – without much reflection – the traditional self-esteem concept. We pursue happiness by making ourselves feel better about our view of ourselves. We want others to see us in a good light too. We rate ourselves against a variety of criteria, and the result is an estimate of our personal view of our value or worth. Experts have noted some of the criteria used by people to enhance their self-esteem. These are listed below:

- good physical attributes
- achievement (e.g. passing exams, holding academic and/or professional qualifications)
- rewarding relationships
- a rewarding career
- owning a top-of-the-range car
- competence in personally significant areas (e.g. Sudoku)
- being a good parent, grandparent, sibling, uncle or aunt
- being a loyal friend or colleague
- being a good partner or lover
- approval from significant others
- being loved by a significant other(s)
- practising a religious faith
- owning land or property.

Let's be realistic, some of our attributes do change over time whether we like it or not. If we rate ourselves in terms of possessing any one of these aspects, when we lose them our self-esteem may drop or even plummet.

There is an alternative. And that alternative is good self-esteem – sometimes known as self-acceptance – in which we rate our attributes (but not ourselves) globally. You can learn – with hard work and practice – to accept yourself, warts and all, and not berate yourself on a regular basis. How is this done?

The first step is to become aware that the architect of your low self-esteem is your Personal Fault Finder (PFF), whose job it is to constantly whisper in your ear, reminding you of your faults and weaknesses. Fear of failure is a favourite topic of conversation for your PFF. It spends a great deal of time telling you not only that you probably *will* fail, but that it will also be untenable if you do. Your PFF's solution is that you are better off not having a go in the first place.

Once you recognize your PFF's undermining and negative view of you and the world, you can start to examine its self-esteem-reducing thinking, challenge it and then modify it. Using established cognitive behavioural techniques (CBT) and strategies you can shift from low self-esteem to good self-esteem and self-acceptance.

Let's consider one simple technique called 'befriending'. Good questions to ask and thereby challenge your PFF are:

▶ 'Would my best friend agree with my negative views of myself?'
▶ 'If not, what might they say about me?'
▶ 'Why would my friend see me differently to the way I see myself?'

You can become your own 'best friend' by using the questions above regularly.

Another technique is to become aware of the trouble that the demanding words, 'should', 'must' and 'ought' can do to your self-esteem. They can develop into absolutist and rigid rules which control your life, such as:

▶ 'I must always perform well.'
▶ 'I must put others' needs before my own needs.'
▶ 'I ought to a perfect parent.'
▶ 'I should always arrive on time.'
▶ 'I should not let people down.'

Begin to look out for these words and phrases that you may use on a regular basis. If you don't live up to such demanding expectations, why not change them to something more realistic and flexible, such as:

- ▶ 'I strongly prefer to perform well but I don't have to.'
- ▶ 'Although I prefer to put others' needs before my own needs, I can choose when and where not to do this.'
- ▶ 'I'm a fallible parent. I will do the best I can and not berate myself if my standards fall.'
- ▶ 'It's strongly desirable to arrive on time, but realistically I may not.'
- ▶ 'It's preferable and desirable not to let people down, but when I do it's more evidence that I'm fallible, that's all.'

To summarize, during our childhood we start to learn how to esteem and disesteem ourselves. It's a way of thinking about our attributes and we tend to globally rate ourselves. For example: 'If I act stupidly then I'm totally stupid.' Good self-esteem and self-acceptance give us permission to stop linking these internal or external attributes to our ego. We learn very quickly that we are no longer defined by our behaviour.

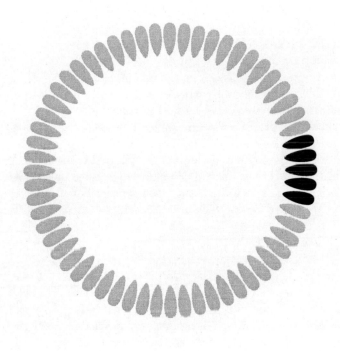

# 10 Only got ten minutes?

Self-esteem is, in essence, a measurement. We rate ourselves against a variety of criteria, and the result is an estimate of our personal view of our value or worth. If we perceive ourselves as doing well by all of our significant criteria or internal scale, then our self-esteem will be high. And conversely, if we perceive ourselves as not doing well then we may disesteem ourselves.

## YOUR PERSONAL FAULT FINDER

The architect of low self-esteem is your Personal Fault Finder (PFF), whose job it is to constantly whisper in your ear, reminding you of your faults and weaknesses, for example: 'You're useless'. Low self-esteem can persist on a personal level – even when you are accomplishing a great deal at an intellectual level – as your PFF works tirelessly to remind you of your faults and weaknesses. You can learn to challenge any fear of failure engendered by your PFF by reminding yourself that there is no such concept as failure unless you choose to believe so. But there are successes and learning experiences.

## SELF-ACCEPTANCE

Self-acceptance is an alternative to the self-esteem trap, as we may rate our attributes but not ourselves globally. Therefore if you fail at a task, it does not mean you are a total failure or worthless or useless as a person. Self-acceptance acknowledges strongly the difference between our person and our behaviour.

## NEGATIVE AUTOMATIC THOUGHTS

Negative Automatic Thoughts (NATs) are the 'top layer' of our thinking: 'I think I've just said the wrong thing' or 'I can tell he doesn't like me'. No reasoning, no pondering or internal debating: purely and simply, the first thought that comes into our head. NATs are easy to believe, unhelpful and difficult to stop.

It is worth learning how to tackle NATs so they do not undermine you.

## NEGATIVE BELIEFS

Negative beliefs are the 'bottom layer' of our thinking. We regard them as absolute – in our minds, they are not open to debate, as we (often erroneously) believe them to be facts. We have negative beliefs about:

▶ ourselves ('I am worthless')
▶ others ('People always let you down')
▶ the world ('Crime is everywhere')
▶ the future ('Nothing will ever change').

Negative beliefs usually develop in our childhood. If we want to develop good self-esteem or greater self-acceptance, as adults we need to start questioning and challenging these core beliefs and then develop positive core beliefs instead.

## NEGATIVE ASSUMPTIONS

Negative assumptions link our beliefs to our day-to-day thinking. In this sense they are the intermediate or 'middle layer' of our thinking. These are sometimes known as underlying negative assumptions and we are not always aware of them.

They have an interesting impact upon us and our behaviour. For example, you may have two associated core beliefs – the positive belief could be 'I am a success'. However, your negative or core belief could be 'I am a total failure'. Whereas you may be happy to activate the positive core belief you will avoid triggering or activating the negative core belief. Following on from these two beliefs the associated positive assumption could be 'If I perform well, then I am a success'. However the downside is the alternative negative assumption 'If I perform badly, then I am a total failure'.

## YOUR RULES FOR LIVING

Rules for living are also intermediate beliefs too. You may develop a rule for living such as 'I must perform well at all times' or 'I should avoid confrontation'. Often they go hand in hand with the negative assumption and negative or core belief. For example:

- ▶ 'I must perform well.' (rule)
- ▶ 'If I don't perform well, then I'm a total failure.' (negative assumption)
- ▶ 'I'm a total failure.' (negative or core belief)

If we comply with our rules for living then we avoid activating our negative beliefs. It's probably one of the key reasons why we actually develop rules over time. However, rules do add pressure to our lives.

### WHAT NEEDS TO BE DONE TO IMPROVE SELF-ESTEEM?

To move from low self-esteem to good self-esteem and greater self-acceptance we need to challenge and modify our:

- ▶ Negative Automatic Thoughts (NATs)
- ▶ underlying negative assumptions and rules
- ▶ negative beliefs.

We then need to develop Positive Activating Thoughts (PATs) – helpful positive assumptions, flexible and preferential rules and positive negative beliefs.

### RECOGNIZING DISTORTED THINKING PATTERNS

Psychologists have identified a number of common thinking errors that most of us make some of the time (and some of us make all of the time). If you know what these are, and recognize

them, it will make challenging rebuttals much easier to formulate.
They include:

## Generalizing the specific
We come to a *general* conclusion based on a *single* incident or
piece of evidence. We use words such as 'always', 'never', 'nobody'
and 'everyone' to make a general rule out of a specific situation.

## Mind reading
Mind reading is one of the commonest thinking errors we make
when our self-esteem is low. This is fatal to self-esteem because we
think that everyone agrees with our negative opinion of ourselves.

## Filtering
We take the negative details from a situation and then magnify
them, while at the same time filtering out all the positive aspects.

## Polarized thinking
We think of situations, people or the world in extremes such as
good or bad: 'I must be perfect or I am a failure.' The problem is
that we usually find ourselves on the negative end of our polarized
extremes.

## Catastrophizing
We predict and expect disaster. We notice or hear about a problem
and immediately decide that if this terrible thing did happen to us,
we would not be able to cope.

## Personalization
This involves thinking that everything people do or say is some
kind of reaction to us; we instantly decide that a comment is really
directed at us personally.

## Blaming
This is the opposite of personalization. We hold other people,
organizations or even the universe responsible for our problems:
'It's all her fault we lost that contract.'

**It's all my fault**
Instead of feeling a victim, we feel responsible for the pain and
happiness of everyone around us.

**Fallacy of fairness**
We feel resentful because we think we know what's fair, but other
people won't agree with us.

Checking out possible thinking errors is another excellent skill to
add to your toolbox. Make sure that you use it regularly.

## SELF-DEFEATING BEHAVIOUR

If a person with low self-esteem gets turned down for a job, their
PFF may say to them: 'You're useless. You will never get a good
job. There will always be other candidates far better than you.'

In this negative thinking state, the likelihood is that their *behaviour*
will mirror their *thinking*. They may even stop applying for jobs at all.
They may still continue to go for interviews but expect to do badly at
them, which will be reflected in the impression they make. This means
that they are likely to remain unemployed – confirming that their
negative thoughts and beliefs were correct. Not only is it important to
challenge and modify our unhelpful thoughts, assumptions and beliefs
but to modify our self-defeating behaviour too.

## PERFECTIONISM

Many people's low self-esteem is driven by unhelpful thinking
about the standards they should be able to reach in order to feel
good about themselves. Demanding that you have to do a perfect
job or be a perfect parent is such a pressure to put yourself under.
A good alternative is to flexibly strive for excellence but not for
rigid and unattainable perfection.

## THINKING AND BEHAVING ASSERTIVELY

Thinking assertively is as important as behaving assertively. It allows you to focus on outcomes and results, rather than simply running with your emotions and 'seeing what happens'. It helps you to maintain your levels of good self-esteem.

### PESSIMISTIC THINKING

Pessimistic thinking reinforces low self-esteem, while optimistic thinking allows us to be more self-accepting and retain a 'feel good' factor in the face of adversity. Yet the only difference between an optimist and a pessimist is their thinking style. We can learn to recognize and then dispute negative (pessimistic) thoughts and put this skill to excellent use in becoming a more optimistic thinker.

### RESILIENCE

Resilience is the ability to adapt well to stress, adversity, trauma or tragedy. It means that overall you remain stable and maintain healthy levels of psychological and physical functioning in the face of disruption or chaos. Resilience can be developed and it will help you to become more secure from within.

## Conclusion

Good self-esteem and greater self-acceptance are very desirable and can be achieved by examining, challenging and modifying our negative beliefs and unhelpful thoughts through using cognitive behavioural techniques.

# Introduction

It doesn't have to take a crisis or negative event to trigger low self-esteem. Some of us feel that we have suffered in this way for most, if not all, of our lives. We may not even be aware of its existence; it can manifest itself in terms of our lack of belief that we can achieve what we want, that people will like us as we wish them to, or that we deserve happiness and fulfilment in our lives.

The fact that you have taken the trouble to purchase and begin to read this book tells us that you probably consider yourself to be suffering from low self-esteem and that you would seriously like to do something about it. Or perhaps you would just like to enhance your self-esteem to new heights.

You have made a good decision. By the time you have worked through all of the sections of this book, you will understand more about the unhelpful thinking and self-defeating behaviour that can lead us down the path of thinking negatively about ourselves. You will discover the confidence to live the life you want and achieve the goals you hope for. You will tackle your PFF. With hard work and practice you will become more accepting of yourself and less dependent upon having to raise your self-esteem to feel good in the first place. You will also learn about the field of positive psychology.

The book contains author insight boxes just like this one, which relate to the section you are reading, providing our insight.

## Insight

It's an interesting and fascinating paradox: the more you accept yourself, the less you will be concerned about self-esteem!

Each chapter provides useful exercises to assist in understanding and tackling low self-esteem, working towards changing how you view yourself. We are aware that this is a heavy workload to ask of you, especially as each section will be accompanied by a practical assignment for you to undertake. However, the benefits will be worthwhile.

You have the choice of dipping into each chapter or starting at Chapter 1, which is the beginning of your self-esteem enhancement programme. To maintain momentum, you may find a daily approach provides the boost you need. Each stage of new learning is accompanied by an exercise to keep you on your toes. The exercises are the most important part of the book, and it is essential that you take them seriously. We will never ask too much of you – sometimes they will require you to do little more than ensure you really understand your learning from a particular step by checking it out.

## Insight

To help you fight low self-esteem it is essential to undertake the exercises that provide insight and assist in changing negative thinking and self-defeating behaviour.

There is something further to add about the exercises. They are not always 'one offs'. Several of the points will be ongoing. This is because you will only internalize your new, more confident way of being by making your exercises your new 'default'. We are also looking for patterns that are personal to you, and this kind of detective work only succeeds when you have a good many samples to analyse – as you will come to appreciate as you work on the tasks.

The good news is that, as we emphasize in other parts of the book, nothing that we ask of you will take too long nor will it be too difficult.

---

## How to use this book

First, you need some tools. Do ensure that, before you start, you have purchased two books – preferably hardcover A4 lined pads – own a whole clutch of working pens and have a safe, quiet personal place to keep them where they will not be pilfered by other members of the family or colleagues at work. We ask you to use hardcover pads as this will definitely give more cohesiveness to the confidence-building work you are about to undertake. If you use five-in-a-pack cheap pads, you are far more likely to mislay them, find someone else has taken them or use a different (but similar-looking) one by mistake; this will mean you either lose a lot of your good work, or have it stored all over the place in different workbooks and your momentum may well go. Of course, some readers may prefer to keep notes on their computer or mobile phone notepad instead as this may be more convenient and immediately accessible.

Once you have your tools to hand, take a look at the layout of this book. It is divided into 12 chapters, each dealing with a different aspect of self-confidence. Some will be more relevant to your own life and ideas than others, so you may wish to focus on those aspects that seem most closely to reflect your own problems.

In a nutshell, cognitive behavioural therapy (CBT) and coaching works by helping you to modify your unhelpful thinking and behaviours. This process helps you to achieve your realistic goals.

We can promise you now that:

> ▶ *confidence-building will be interesting*
> ▶ *we will spell things out in a punchy, common sense way that you will grasp speedily and easily*
> ▶ *you will see excellent results quickly*
> ▶ *you will become an expert on the skills to increase confidence, which will hopefully last a life time.*
> ▶ *we will stay alongside you every step of the way*
> ▶ *life will be so much better by the end of all your hard work!*

So, let's go!

# 1

# Great self-esteem: what is it?

In this chapter you will learn:
- *what self-esteem – or lack of it – is*
- *the possible origins of your own low self-esteem*
- *how your 'Personal Fault Finder' deceives you*
- *the value of self-acceptance*
- *how to set goals to improve your self-esteem.*

## What is self-esteem?

What do we mean when we talk about self-esteem? You will probably agree that it includes some, or all, of the following:

- ▶ *the ability to enjoy life to the full*
- ▶ *the ability to cope with life's ups and downs*
- ▶ *feeling good about ourselves*
- ▶ *feeling that others, in general, like us*
- ▶ *having a positive attitude*
- ▶ *having good social skills*
- ▶ *the willingness to give new things a go*
- ▶ *the willingness to take risks*
- ▶ *the ability to make difficult decisions*
- ▶ *the ability to achieve life goals.*

Self-esteem can best be described as having confidence in your own abilities and values. It does not mean thinking that you are the best at everything, but feeling comfortable with yourself even when you are not. It is accepting yourself, with all your strengths and weaknesses, while still taking opportunities for self-development.

In simple terms therefore, self-esteem means having trust and faith in yourself. Before you can do this however, you need to like and value yourself. You also need to be able to accept yourself as you are. The 'catch 22' situation here is that, if your self-esteem is low then these are tall orders.

### A MEASUREMENT

Self-esteem is, in essence, a measurement. We rate ourselves against a variety of criteria, and the result is an estimate of our personal view of our value or worth. The problem is that we tend to rate ourselves very inaccurately and very harshly. This in turn leads to low self-esteem, since based on our negative perceptions, we continue to undervalue ourselves. Worse is to come – once a person believes something to be true, he or she will start to *act* as if it were. The person will start to gather evidence to support this erroneous belief, while at the same time discounting evidence that fails to support it, thus strengthening the negative view of his or her personal value.

## Insight

This is the self-esteem trap. Many of us fall into it. We measure our self-esteem through subjectively rating ourselves – usually harshly and negatively. We need to be aware that this can lead us to live with low self-esteem based on unhelpful information and reasoning – not truths or facts.

## Exercise

Think about a time when you felt really confident – perhaps you had done something well, or someone had praised you.

▶ *Did you need a particular achievement to give you this positive feeling?*

> ▶ *Can you remember having such a feeling without having
> excelled at anything special or receiving any particular
> positive input?*

## Childhood origins

Where does our low self-esteem come from? Are we born with it?
Is it genetic? Do we learn it? Have life events simply conspired
against us so that we feel everything we do goes wrong, and we
never get that lucky 'break' that would give our confidence a boost?

Most people suffer from some element of low self-esteem. Problems
usually develop when our self-esteem plummets so low that it
starts preventing us from doing things: 'I'm not trying for the job
promotion – I'll never get it anyway' or 'I didn't invite so-and-so
to go out with me – they would be sure to say no, and then I'd feel
even worse about myself'.

Where does this come from? Finally, a chance to blame the parents!
Parents often feel that criticism encourages their child to be aware
of their weaknesses and therefore try harder to improve.

Parents may feel that their own views, built on knowledge and
experience, are to be passed down to their offspring. So a child
may learn that what they think is 'wrong' while what someone
else (their parent) thinks is 'right'. For example: a father who says
'You idiot' when his son makes an error will scarcely recollect
saying it, while the child absorbs the idea that he is an 'idiot'.

We can see how the low self-esteem habit can develop – and this is
in caring and well-adjusted households. Now consider how many
children grow up in households where they are regularly vilified,
ridiculed and abused.

Then there is school to contend with. Woe betide you if you:

▶ *wear glasses*
▶ *have red hair*
▶ *are slightly overweight or undersized*
▶ *wear the wrong make of trainers*
▶ *don't belong to the right gang*
▶ *struggle with maths and are admonished by the teacher in front of your classmates*
▶ *are poor at sports and always come last in competitive events.*

Can you begin to see how hard it is for any of us to grow up feeling particularly good about ourselves?

## Insight

Low self-esteem tends to develop during our childhoods. Even where we have had a relatively happy time of it, we can still absorb, and carry with us into adulthood, negative thoughts about ourselves through parental criticism.

Think about the lessons you learned in your childhood. For example, if you are shy with strangers, think about the opportunities you had (or did not have) to talk to adults in such a way that you felt an 'equal' rather than simply a child. If you find it hard to stand up to people, think about how your parents reacted if you 'rebelled' in any way. Look at the characteristics you consider personal weaknesses, and see if you can find a point in your childhood where these ideas might have begun.

This may help you to understand how your low self-esteem gradually developed.

## Adulthood: time to tackle low self-esteem

What we would like you to recognize is that the corrosive power of low self-esteem comes largely from external circumstances. This is natural.

A concept that will help you overcome this is self-acceptance. When you adopt the idea of self-acceptance, you begin to value yourself *in spite of what others think*. In the examples we gave you previously, low self-esteem has developed, in the main, due to the negative views and comments of significant others in our lives. If we can develop enough resilience to value ourselves in spite of what others may think, we will begin to feel much better about ourselves.

This is a journey to be learned in adulthood by most of us, and requires us to work to change the view that we have of ourselves that we have carried from childhood. In Chapter 2 you will learn exactly how to banish these negative thoughts that may have haunted you for a long time.

## A WOBBLY BIKE

Self-esteem is a rickety bicycle in that it wobbles a great deal. If your mood drops, so can your self-esteem and vice versa. You can also feel especially confident in certain areas of your life – super confident even – and yet hopelessly inadequate in others. Some people say to us: 'I am completely confident in my workplace, but seem unable to sustain any sort of personal relationship and feel a total failure in this area.'

## NEGATIVE SELF-RATING

Low self-esteem can result in depression and having thoughts that you are 'worthless' or even that you are a 'bad' person. We tend to define these negative responses by using a comparative rating system. For example, we may decide that someone we know is our idea of a 'perfect' person and we compare ourselves very unfavourably against this paragon. We also tend to give ourselves 'global' ratings, for example: 'So-and-so is a much better person than I am', rather than specific ratings 'So-and-so is more attractive than me, but I can play the piano better' which would be more realistic.

> **Insight**
> Developing the idea of liking ourselves 'no matter what'
> will give us a much stronger base for self-esteem than being
> dependent on our achievements and external feed-in.

Can you identify any personal characteristics or behaviours where you genuinely believe, 'This is me and other people can like it or lump it?' Think about these characteristics for a moment. Are you more confident when you take this view? If so, these are genuine beliefs. If not, you are probably masking low self-esteem with defiance.

### WHAT MAINTAINS LOW SELF-ESTEEM?

In our daily lives, most of us experience many events that make us feel good about ourselves. We get good jobs, enter into loving relationships and create reasonably satisfying lives. So why does low self-esteem plague some of us?

The answer is the beliefs that we have about ourselves that have developed over many years. The mistake we make is to confuse these beliefs with facts.

> **Insight**
> We cannot stress strongly enough the importance of grasping
> this point, and keeping it in your mind. We can change
> beliefs, but we cannot change facts.

CASE STUDY

## Melissa's story

Melissa was a bright student at school. However her home life was poor, with an absent father and a mother who escaped her own inadequacies by drinking heavily. When drunk, she became abusive and Melissa bore the brunt of this, for the simple reason that she looked very much like her absent father. When she tried to study at home, her mother told her that her father was stupid, and therefore so was she, so what was the point of studying?

Melissa managed to keep her mother's beliefs at bay until she got low grades in one of her tests. For the first time, she began to wonder if what her mother told her was true. She then feared her next test, as she realized that – in her own perceptions – perhaps she *was* rather stupid. Because of this anxiety, Melissa struggled with her next test and did poorly. Melissa now took this as proof that her mother was right. There was no point in trying, as it was a waste of time. Sadly Melissa consequently failed at school and achieved very little in her adult life. However, in Melissa's mind this correctly reflected her low value and status in life, so it never occurred to her to do anything about it.

**Insight**

No matter how much we believe negative aspects of ourselves, that does not necessarily make them true.

**Exercise**

Take one negative belief about yourself, for example: 'I'm hopeless at sport'. Next write down in your notebook where this belief came from.

▶ *What evidence do you have to support it? Write down at least three different pieces of evidence here – one is not enough.*
▶ *Now think about this for a while and then write down any evidence you may have to challenge this view. This can be as simple as, 'To be honest, I've never even tried football, so it is only an assumption that I would be useless at it.'*

Don't worry if you find this difficult at this stage. You are simply learning to stretch your thinking at this point and to appreciate the difference between beliefs and hard facts.

Melissa's story explains how low self-esteem is maintained. Melissa confused a *belief* with a *fact*. When Melissa failed her second test, instead of looking for rational reasons why this might have happened that she could have worked on (for example being over-anxious, misreading a question, not having studying hard enough) she accepted her stupidity as the root cause of her failure, and her failure as evidence of her stupidity.

---

## Introducing your Personal Fault Finder

Low self-esteem prevents you from accepting yourself as a valuable human being. You can achieve a great deal by way of positive accomplishments in your life, and still suffer from low self-esteem. This is because there is a difference between an acceptance of your abilities on an intellectual level, and an acceptance of yourself on a personal level.

The architect of your low self-esteem is your Personal Fault Finder (PFF), whose job it is to constantly whisper in your ear, reminding you of your faults and weaknesses. Use your imagination to imagine what your PFF looks like. (Although this may sound childish, bear with us, it is actually a very helpful tool.) What about a pantomime character – tall and thin, in an ill-fitting suit and a huge top hat? Or a little gremlin that sits on your shoulder chattering away to you? Or perhaps an animal – or a radio you can't seem to switch off? You might even want to give your PFF a name. Using imagery in this way will help you to view your critical self as something (or someone) external to yourself that you don't need to keep listening to. In turn, it will be much easier for you to fight something you can visualize and whom you can tell to 'get lost' as your self-esteem improves.

> ### Insight
> Low self-esteem can persist on a personal level, even when we are accomplishing a great deal at an intellectual level as our Personal Fault Finder (PFF) works tirelessly to remind us of our faults and weaknesses.

Once bedded in, your PFF is very hard to dislodge. You learn to live with it and trust and believe what it says. One of the main goals of this book is to enable you to remove your PFF and see it for the fraud that it is. With a little work, this is quite achievable and you will be amazed at how differently you will view yourself without your PFF around to demoralize you.

## Exercise

Conjure up a description of your Personal Fault Finder.

▶ *Make it as colourful as you can. The more you bring imagery into play here, the easier it will be for you to deal with your inner critic. Make the caricature humorous, which will also be helpful.*
▶ *Now replay in your mind that last critical comment 'he' or 'she' made. Does imagining your PFF in this way help you to loosen the extent to which you believe the criticism?*

### HOW YOUR PFF ENCOURAGES YOU TO RELY ON ITS UNTRUTHS

Your PFF is a dangerous friend. Not only is it able to constantly remind you of perceived weaknesses, failures and inabilities – it also encourages you to believe that it is actually protecting you from harm. In turn, your self-esteem becomes even lower – and your PFF has us just where it wants you.

The following examples may be familiar to you.

▶ *Your PFF constantly reminds you that you are useless, worthless and valueless. These thoughts are so upsetting and painful, that finding a way to relieve them becomes vital. But how? The answer your PFF has up its sleeve is to set very*

*high goals for yourself. Surely, if you can gain workplace*
*promotion, become the perfect partner, lose weight, look*
*fantastic, become good at a new hobby or interest, then –*
*your PFF tells you – you will stop thinking negatively about*
*yourself. Relying on these impossible goals to make you feel*
*better, you consistently fail and your self-esteem plummets*
*even lower.*

▶ *Your PFF tells you that others will probably reject you and*
*that it will be very painful. The solution is to predict your*
*rejection in advance, and therefore take steps to avoid it*
*happening. Your PFF helps you to predict this rejection by*
*telling you: 'You won't get the promotion and it will be*
*completely humiliating – best not to even go for it'; 'If you*
*say anything at the committee meeting, others will see what*
*little grasp you have of the facts. Perhaps it would be best to*
*resign?'; 'You can tell that your lover is losing interest –*
*he was looking at the TV guide while you were speaking*
*to him. It's obviously over, so why not ditch him first?'*

Your PFF encourages you to feel that avoiding rejection is better
than experiencing it. The downside is, of course, that you fail to see
that your negative predictions may have been wrong – you might
have got the job, become Chairperson of the committee, settled
down with your lover, who knows?

## Insight

Your PFF not only feeds you negative information, it offers
solutions that are tempting to you since they reduce your
anxiety and assist you in avoidance of perceived difficult
situations. However, while reducing anxiety, it also
reduces your self-esteem and reinforces your negative
perceptions.

Think about an area of your life where your confidence is low.
What is your PFF telling you? What solutions does it come up
with? How do these affect you? Does your self-esteem increase as a
result of taking your PFF's advice? If not, why not? Doing this will

increase your awareness of the way your PFF disguises its sabotage as 'help'.

## FEAR OF FAILURE: YOUR PFF'S FORTE

Fear of failure is a favourite topic of conversation for your PFF. It spends a great deal of time telling you not only that you probably *will* fail but that it will also be untenable if you do. The PFF's solution is that you are better off not having a go in the first place.

Imagine learning to ski and being told you are good enough to go up into the next class. Your PFF immediately steps in and questions this: Supposing that isn't true? Supposing you can't cope, fall, injure yourself or make an idiot of yourself? You begin to feel really anxious about improving your skiing. Perhaps you would be better not to give it a go as you may fail? Yes, that is the answer. Don't even bother. Stay with the beginners group. How do you feel now? Relaxed – the anxiety is gone. What a relief! But you are still no good at skiing, and now you never will be. No chance of increased self-esteem in this area – you will forever recount to friends how you found you were 'No good at skiing'.

---

## The importance of risk taking

The saying 'To risk nothing is to risk everything' is very powerful. We must learn to assess risk, manage risk and take risk – or we will never move forward in life. It's beneficial to learn that there is no such thing as failure – there are only successes and learning experiences. It simply doesn't matter if we are not the best at everything or sometimes make mistakes. But your PFF won't let you see things this way, in case you make some positive discoveries about yourself. So it heightens your anxiety and fear of failing to the point that it seems quite unbearable for you to do so. Your PFF achieves this by running you down, then offering 'solutions' that appear to help but which, in fact, put the nail in your self-esteem coffin.

Your PFF is a false friend, and in the course of this book you will learn to silence it for ever.

> ## Insight
> Challenge any fear of failure engendered by your PFF by reminding yourself that there is no such concept as failure unless you choose to believe so. But there are successes and learning experiences.

Can you think of any examples in your own life where your fear of failure has prevented you from achievement? Looking back, how do you feel about that now? Now consider two or three times when you were very afraid, but undertook the task or faced the fear anyway. How did you feel afterwards if you gave it a go and failed? How did you feel afterwards if you succeeded? Which of these three feelings was the most positive? Which was the least positive? Why?

## The consequences of low self-esteem

One of the saddest aspects of low self-esteem is that it tends to alienate us from others. We may believe that we have so little value that it is not worth making an effort with people, or we tend to take on a 'victim' mantle, where we feel that life has been very unfair to us. Here are some common examples of how low self-esteem can affect how we think and behave. Notice any that you recognize in yourself.

### It's everyone else
We tend to blame other people for our misfortunes: 'I would not have done this, if he had not said that.' We decide that we have been unfairly treated, without considering why. We absorb 'magic' ideas, such as: 'All the bad things always happen to me.' The more inadequate we feel, the more critical we become – it is as though finding fault with others helps us build ourselves up.

**Pay attention to me!**
Sufferers of low self-esteem rely on feed-in from others to make themselves feel good. They feel miffed and upset if this attention is not forthcoming. For example, one partner at a party being berated by the other partner for not paying them enough attention while spending a lot of time talking to others. This is low self-esteem talking.

**Selfishness**
Low self-esteem can breed selfishness. We become so self-absorbed, so wrapped up in our own needs and desires that we have little time to consider the needs and interests of others, even those we love and care for.

**Coffee or tea?**
We are so uncertain of our ability to make a good decision that we dither, procrastinate and become totally indecisive. This can lead to poor decision making skills, which in turn reinforce the person's low self-esteem.

**Poor me**
This is the 'victim mentality' we referred to at the start of the section. It can manifest itself in two ways:

▶ *First, we tell ourselves that we are the victims of circumstances that are outside our control, which prevents us from taking responsibility for what is happening and does actually allow other people to push us around a bit.*
▶ *Second, we may even find comfort in being a victim. It's what we are used to. We believe it will make people feel sorry for us, and therefore pay us more attention.*

**Boastfulness**
When we think we are inadequate compared to those around us, we may attempt to rectify this by overdoing things in the wrong way. For example, we may name drop, refer to recent personal success stories or affect unnatural mannerisms in the way

we speak. The idea is to impress others and make them think more of us. In reality, we do ourselves a disservice and impress no one.

## Over-competitiveness

Our need to be right all the time stems from a desperate need to prove ourselves to those around us. Logically, it is extraordinary to believe that beating everyone else at everything would give us more acceptance and approval from others. Yet this is a form that low self-esteem can take for many people.

These are just some (although not all) of the ways that, in our attempts to increase our self-esteem, we end up lowering it even further. Please don't think of yourself as an outcast if you recognize some of these traits. We have all been guilty of some of these things at one time or another. That is human nature. It is the *extent* to which we behave in these ways which can blight our lives.

We need to learn to accept ourselves as being just fine as we are in order to get rid of these negative traits. It isn't nearly as difficult as you might think.

## Exercise

▶ *Do you consider that any of the above traits apply to you? Be really honest.*
▶ *How many of these traits ring a bell with you?*

Don't feel defensive about this – we all tend, from time to time, to attempt to boost our self-esteem using inappropriate tools. But it is very important to recognize what we do, and to acknowledge it, before we can start to correct it.

# Introducing self-acceptance

Can you think of anyone you know who treats everyone else as an equal and usually says exactly what is in his mind? A person who appears confident but not arrogant? A person who seems to keep any mistakes that they make in perspective, who can listen or talk, work or relax, and seems constantly at ease?

You might say – if you have someone in mind – that this friend has high self-esteem or is very confident. Yet what we are actually describing here is a much more valuable commodity – that of self-acceptance. This person is one who accepts herself entirely as she is, and does not waste precious time worrying about what she is not. She still strives to achieve what she wants from life and to live it to her best abilities, but she does not constantly compare herself with others who do more, or beat herself up when she tries and fails, or makes mistakes.

Doesn't that sound a good way to be? Would you also like to be like that? You can learn how.

## FEELING GOOD WITHOUT FEELING BAD

If we can only feel good about ourselves when someone else praises us, or when we get a job promotion, this leaves us in dire straits when we get criticized or ignored, or passed over for the job we want.

Self-acceptance will come to our rescue. We can make the distinction between valuing ourselves as a person, no matter what, and accepting that being a fallible human being who messes up from time to time is quite okay. This is the heart of self-acceptance. If we fail at a task it does not mean we are a total failure. If we act stupidly it does not make us a stupid person. Self-acceptance acknowledges strongly the difference between our person and our behaviour.

We will be incorporating the ideas of self-acceptance into this book alongside self-esteem; this will give your view of yourself an extra stability, no matter what the external circumstances.

## Insight

Not feeling badly about yourself is just as vital as feeling good about yourself. This is one aspect of self-acceptance, and is valuable as it is a permanent state, not one that fluctuates according to how the outside world is treating you at any given moment. It is therefore a commodity well worth developing.

## Exercise: testing your self-esteem levels

Even when we feel our self-esteem is very low, some of these negative feelings come from discounting our strengths and abilities, rather than not having any.

▶ *Read and consider the statements below. Mark each statement on a scale of 0 to 4, according to the level you agree or disagree with it, where:*

0 = never
1 = agree occasionally
2 = agree sometimes
3 = agree most of the time
4 = totally agree

▶ *When you've completed the test, add up your scores.*

1 *I consider myself to be a fairly worthwhile person.*
2 *I can take criticism reasonably well.*
3 *I don't take remarks people make too personally.*
4 *I attempt to encourage myself rather than criticize myself for my weaknesses.*

5   When I make mistakes, I don't see myself as a total failure.
6   I expect most people to like me.
7   I am socially confident.
8   I make some contribution to society, even if only a small one.
9   It doesn't especially upset me if others disagree with my views.
10  While being aware of my shortcomings I actually quite like myself.
11  I feel that my life is fairly well on track.
12  I can usually deal positively with setbacks.
13  I attempt not to compare myself with others.
14  I have a sense of humour and can laugh at myself.
15  I generally consider that life is interesting and fun.

## Score

*A perfect 60*
You *may* have a problem! Self-esteem that is too high can be as dysfunctional as self-esteem that is too low. Alternatively, wow, well done!

*45–59*
Why are you reading this book?! Of course, you can still gain useful insight.

*30–44*
You certainly need a boost, but you recognize some of your good points, so making positive adjustments should not be too difficult for you.

*15–29*
You are suffering unnecessarily from negative thinking about yourself. We hope that will have changed totally by the time you have worked through this book.

*(Contd)*

*0–14*

You have a very serious self-esteem problem. This book may be enough to help you, but if not, you might benefit from professional assistance.

▶ *Now look at the test again. Were you perhaps rather hard on yourself? This is a common feature of low self-esteem.*

▶ *Consider your answers one more time, thinking of any instances when you have perhaps felt a little more positive than you initially thought. Avoid just focusing on the negative.*

## WHAT IS A WORTHWHILE HUMAN BEING?

The first question we asked you to consider in the last step was whether you believe you are a worthwhile human being.

Is your idea of a person who is worthwhile someone who is kind to others, makes a contribution to society, is devoted to their family? Possibly, one who has a spiritual or religious leaning, who has been successful career-wise, has created financial stability and shares this with others?

In other words, quite a paragon of virtue!

Is it any wonder that if we set one of our personal goals as being 'worthwhile' we could be aiming to achieve the equivalent of climbing Mount Everest without oxygen?

**You already have value**
One of the goals of this book is to encourage you to realize that you are someone of great value just because you exist. While you will learn to make positive changes, these will be to *enhance* your self worth, not to *create* it.

A little earlier, we also mentioned the fact that self-esteem can be too high, and this is as detrimental as low self-esteem. Why do you think this might be?

## Overblown self-esteem

We see all around us the results of people whose overblown sense of self-esteem (which we may call self-importance) has caused their downfall. Apart from many of the prison population, who are often there because they consider themselves above the law – more important than the people they have robbed or harmed, or who somehow find humour in causing misfortune to others – there are endless disgraced politicians, sports stars and other well-known celebrities who have been so convinced of their superiority that they have underestimated the worth, intelligence and moral values held by others in assessing their actions and deeds.

Aim to feel happy with yourself in spite of your weaknesses, and you will like yourself just as much as someone who scored 60 on the test in the last step. But, more importantly, others will like you a great deal more – and you won't end up on the front pages of the newspapers for the wrong reasons!

## Insight

You are already a very worthwhile person just because you exist. You simply need to learn to believe it – too much self-esteem is less attractive than simply accepting yourself 'warts and all'.

How far do you consider that you might already be worthwhile? Begin to focus on your present assets, not your future goals.

## The hidden benefits of low self-esteem

Jim's story

Peter worked hard to establish his own painting and decorating business. He owned a spacious flat and had a good social life. Then an old friend of his got in touch, telling Peter that he was out of

*(Contd)*

work and looking for somewhere to stay on a temporary basis. Out of past friendship, Peter immediately invited Jim to stay with him while he got back on his feet.

But Jim did not get back on his feet. Having been turned down for a few job interviews, he got discouraged and felt he was unemployable. Jim told Peter that he had no confidence with girls, so Peter introduced Jim to his friends and attempted to set him up on some dates. Jim told Peter that he would love to go on holiday but feeling so low about himself he just didn't have the confidence to ask anyone – and then of course, there was the cost as well... Peter again felt sorry for Jim and offered to go away with him himself and to foot the bill for them both.

By now, Jim was so settled into the flat, he was treating it as his own. He had no bills to pay, an easy life, was failing to develop any social skills – Jim shied away from mixing as he felt others would make him feel inadequate – and above all, he had a friend who worried about him and catered to most of his needs.

This is one of many examples of the *perceived benefits* of low self-esteem. Provided we play the victim, we find that others will feel sorry for us, will rescue us and smooth our path through life. Being a victim can be quite predatory – we tend to hunt down those whom we feel will give us the best response to our sorry tale and focus on trying to get them to help us out.

We ask you to recognize this possibility and learn to honestly identify it if you find yourself using low self-esteem to gain attention or sympathy.

## Insight

There can be a 'pay off' for staying in the low self-esteem zone, if we can use it to encourage sympathy and attention from others. The downside of this is that we never develop self-reliance and a positive thinking style that will help us to accept ourselves without this sort of external input.

# Your personal view of yourself

A phenomenon of life – as many people comment to us (and we have experienced ourselves) – is how long it takes to build up some sort of reasonable self-confidence or 'okay-ness' about ourselves, and how in only a few seconds we can lose all our gains and feel bad about ourselves again.

We can be swinging along the road quite happily, feeling great, excited about the day ahead and then, guess what? We inadvertently catch sight of our reflection in a shop window. Suddenly we see that our hair looks a mess, our nose is too long; the general impression is just not great. The spring goes out of our step and we start ruminating about our lack of attractiveness. Our confidence drains away and the day doesn't seem so exciting and full of potential any more.

Does this sound familiar? Why do you think this happens? Your Personal Fault Finder is at work again.

The reason that it is so powerful is that it is hard at work all the time. It rarely takes a break or goes on holiday. Because it works all day every day, you become conditioned to believe this inner critic. Your PFF defines how you see yourself. Therefore you will only feel good about yourself if you can silence it or block it out somehow. This is possible up to a point. You may feel that you can prove it wrong by achieving something positive, for example losing weight, winning a competition, receiving praise at work or wearing a designer outfit that you know looks good. But these feel-good factors only last for so long.

This is because they are external factors. Your PFF is not in charge of 'externals'. It is in charge of your view of yourself.

Please ensure that you understand this very important point: your PFF ensures that you are *conditioned* to think negatively about yourself, which is why it is so hard to gain confidence and so very easy to lose it again. You won't defeat your PFF by constantly achieving external successes to countermand it, but by becoming so comfortable with yourself that it is rendered useless and disappears.

Think back over the last two weeks and a time when you felt really good about yourself. How long did that feeling last? Did any negative thoughts about yourself bring your mood back down again? Did you actually feel that it was more 'normal' to feel less confident in yourself? If so, you are stuck in a low self-esteem rut, and have been neatly placed there by your PFF.

## Exercise: testing your personal view of yourself

Here is a test that we give to many of our clients, half of which they find easy, and half of which they find very difficult. We will leave you to guess which half is which! This test is your activity for the step, so if you wish to set it aside until you have at least 15 minutes of free time, do so.

First, make sure you have your notebook and pen to hand. Now take your watch off your wrist and set it beside you. We need you to time yourself as you do this test, so don't start until you have made a note of the start time. For the first part of this test, start now.

▶ *List your top ten weaknesses or faults.*
▶ *Stop the clock! How long did that take you? Make a note.*
▶ *Now start the clock again, and complete the second part of the test.*
▶ *List your top ten qualities and strengths.*
▶ *Stop the clock again. Record your time taken.*

What have you discovered? We suspect that you found the first part of the test much easier than the second part.

You may have been inundated with ideas for the first part of the test, yet were scratching about to find ten points for the second part.

Your time record will show that you took a great deal longer to complete the second part of the test than the first.

What does this tell you? That you are a person with hundreds of faults and few good qualities? Or that your view of yourself is defined by a negative thinking style that you may actually be aware of, but feel unable to do anything about?

The second view is almost certainly going to be the real problem, but you know what? It actually doesn't matter whether you believe either the first or the second view.

All that matters is that you are comfortable with yourself – *however you are*. This is the core concept that you will learn as you work through this book. Once you begin to truly accept yourself, you will start to like yourself as well. Life is as good as your relationship with yourself.

---

## Goal setting

Before moving on, research has found that it is important to set goals in order to achieve change. This may seem a slightly strange suggestion after we have spent much of this chapter discussing the idea of being 'okay as you are' and accepting yourself, rather than relentlessly trying to change things.

However, feeling okay – and having good self-acceptance – does not mean that we give up on achieving goals; it simply means that we are still perfectly acceptable people if we don't achieve them, rather than useless duffers. To illustrate this, it is hard to beat the lines from Rudyard Kipling's famous poem 'If':

> *If you can meet with triumph and disaster, and treat these two impostors just the same...*

Good self-esteem isn't about winning all the time. It is about being gracious in defeat. It is about accepting yourself even when you lose – and using the loss as part of the learning curve, rather than retiring in despair.

There is also a difference between improving your *skills* (for which you may need a book to teach you exactly what it is you wish to improve – 'Beginner's Bridge' or 'How to Win at Rugby') and improving your *self*, which means learning to like yourself more. You will need to make some alterations and adjustments in order to do this, but they will have little to do with achievements and everything to do with creating a heart and a soul that you enjoy spending time with – and which belongs to you.

Thinking less about improving your skills and more about improving your self – which may mean your perceptions of yourself – will help you to set worthwhile self-esteem goals.

Have you already had any ideas about how you might improve your self-esteem? What are they? Do they include improving skills and abilities? If so, review those ideas now.

## Exercise: defining your goals

Here is a question – well-known as the 'miracle question' – which makes goal setting much easier.

*If we could promise you that when you wake up tomorrow you will no longer have low self-esteem, but will feel very confident about yourself, how would you know that this had happened? What changes would you notice in yourself (or in others) that would make it clear that our promise to you had been kept?*

Using your notebook, write down your answer to this question. Come up with at least five things that would be immediately different for you. The answers should highlight your own personal goals. For example, if you wrote 'I would be able to talk to the attractive women at the bus stop', then a personal goal might be:

▶ *'I would like to find it easier to socialize with people I don't know'* or
▶ *'I would like to find a stable and meaningful relationship'* or
▶ *'I would like to have more self-confidence in all situations'.*

If you wrote 'My boss would praise my contribution to the department a great deal more', then a personal goal might be:

▶ *'I would like to achieve more in my career'* or
▶ *'I would like to have more confidence in the quality of the work I produce'* or
▶ *'I would like to think of myself as successful in the workplace'.*

If you wrote, 'I would receive more compliments about my looks', then a personal goal might be:

▶ *'I would like to feel better about my body image'* or
▶ *'I would like to make more effort to look nice'* or
▶ *'I would like to dress more attractively'.*

In your notebook, write down four major personal goals that you would like to achieve with improved self-esteem.

*(Contd)*

Do not write down more than four; it's not necessary. Once you have achieved these four, you will have mastered the skills to enable you to achieve all of your goals with less difficulty. This is because goal setting is about giving you a personal focus – something to aim for. In reality, the skills you will learn will be generic – that is, applicable in any situation, so you do not need to specify them all now. It won't matter!

The skills you will learn will enable your self-esteem to be robust and solid in all situations, not just those you have focused on.

We hope that this first chapter will have given you a good idea of where low self-esteem comes from, what maintains it and the consequences – and even benefits – of suffering from it.

You have made the acquaintance of your PFF, and are keen to shake it off. You have begun to realize that your opinions about yourself may be historically learned and skewed, and that they do not necessarily provide a fair reflection of your self worth.

Importantly, we hope you will have grasped that self-acceptance will kill low self-esteem stone dead.

You are starting to set goals for yourself that will help you to become more confident – the person you would like to be.

# 10 THINGS TO REMEMBER

1   *Self-esteem is a measurement based on our own or others' criteria of what's good.*

2   *Low self-esteem tends to stem from childhood (even in a happy environment).*

3   *We measure our self-esteem through subjectively rating ourselves – usually harshly and negatively.*

4   *Recognize your Personal Fault Finder and start to put him in his place.*

5   *Recognize the consequences of low self-esteem and learn to avoid them.*

6   *Through the power of self-acceptance, you can value yourself as a person, while accepting that it's okay to mess up sometimes.*

7   *An overblown sense of self-esteem (which we may call self-importance) can be as damaging as low self-esteem.*

8   *Be aware (and beware) that sometimes low self-esteem can be used to gain attention or sympathy – the 'poor me' syndrome.*

9   *Don't try to defeat your PFF by constantly striving for external successes to countermand it.*

10  *Recognize the importance of defining and setting your own goals.*

# 2

# Thinking your way out of low self-esteem

In this chapter you will learn:
- *to identify how low self-esteem affects you personally*
- *the common characteristics of negative thinking*
- *how assumptions and rules for living keep our unhelpful beliefs in place*
- *that low self-esteem is not generated by adverse events, but by the way we interpret these events*
- *powerful ways of combating self-defeating thinking.*

## Identifying the problem

Low self-esteem can be caused by a succession of failures, for which we blame ourselves, or a chronic 'drip, drip' of having been told throughout our childhoods that we're not up to much. Then as adults we look for evidence to confirm this idea and not disqualify it.

For some, it has been an all-pervading part of their lives for as long as they can remember. For others, good self-esteem was taken for granted, until an event – or series of events – changed all that. We work with many people who say: 'I used to feel fine about myself. Then that all changed...' They will usually identify:

- ▶ *a time frame ('...two years ago')*
- ▶ *an event ('...when a relationship broke up')*
- ▶ *a period in their lives ('...when I went to university').*

Take a moment to think about your view of your own low self-esteem. Is it generalized? Have you always felt this way – or can you point to a specific time, period or event in your life when you first lost your natural self-confidence?

The answer to this question will help you to identify whether your problem is unhelpful thinking or unhelpful beliefs.

## UNHELPFUL THINKING

This is where you have taken a negative view of events that have befallen you and incorporated these thoughts into your day-to-day thinking style. For example, you have always thought of yourself as attractive until someone you care for deeply ends a relationship, when you decide you must be unlovable; or you always considered yourself as intelligent until you failed an exam, when you realized that you were not so smart.

## UNHELPFUL BELIEFS

This is where our opinion of ourselves is defined by more absolute views – usually developed in childhood – which we consider to be facts. For example: 'I am a selfish person'; 'I cannot get on with others'; 'I'll never make a success of my life'.

Don't worry too much which you believe your problem to be – you may even think it is a mixture of the two. You will still be able to get rid of your Personal Fault Finder just as easily.

## Exercise

Consider where you feel your low self-esteem might come from, and what form it might take, for example: a response to a specific adverse event, or something you feel has simply always been there. Write down now what conclusion you came to.

▶ *If you used to feel okay about yourself, what changed that?*
▶ *If you have always felt poorly about yourself, what beliefs do you actually have?*

The examples we gave you on the previous page should help you.

## The different levels of thinking

*You can transcend all negativity when you realize that the only power it has over you is your belief in it.*

Eileen Caddy

To learn how to feel good about yourself, you need to learn a little about the way your mind operates.

When you are feeling down and have doubts, people often tell you to 'think positively' and 'look on the bright side'. Imagine if it were as easy as that?! Do you sometimes feel like responding, 'Look, I would if I could'? Or do you sometimes agree – and actually attempt to do as you have been advised?

On the basis of this advice, we can simply say to ourselves, over and over 'I am *not* selfish' or 'I am *very* attractive' and our self-esteem should increase in relation to how often we repeat these mantras.

Why do you think this does not work? The answer lies in the fact that our thoughts won't hold any water if they are in direct contradiction to our basic beliefs about ourselves. These beliefs are not *necessarily* true (although they might be) but we *think* they are – which becomes the problem. You could have film star good looks, but if you believe 'I have a big nose that makes my face look ugly', then it really doesn't matter how many times you look in the mirror and repeat to yourself that you are good looking, you're wasting your time. You will never believe this mantra! So don't do that!

---

## Beliefs versus facts

You need to begin to check out whether your beliefs are actually true. Do you really have a big nose, or is that what you see when you look in the mirror because someone at school once rudely suggested that you had?

### MAKING ERRONEOUS ASSUMPTIONS

Does your nose *really* make you look ugly or is that an *assumption* you have made: 'If I have a big nose then I must be ugly'?

Sometimes, our beliefs are right – in which case we can problem solve to make realistic changes. But challenging our beliefs – 'playing detective' to check their validity – is always the first port of call.

## Insight

The age-old advice simply to 'think positively' isn't going to work when your self-esteem is low. Learning to take a second look at your thoughts and beliefs to see how valid they really are is going to be far more helpful in shifting your thinking into a more realistic, positive mode, and your self-esteem into higher gear.

## Exercise

▶ *Do you ever attempt to 'think positively' when your mind is flooded with self-defeating negativity?*
▶ *Does it work for you?*
▶ *Consider when it makes a difference and when it doesn't.*

When you have read to the end of this chapter, return to this point and see if you can give yourself a clearer explanation as to why this rarely works.

## Negative thoughts, assumptions and beliefs

We have now mentioned negative thoughts, negative assumptions and negative beliefs. What is the difference between them? In defeating low self-esteem, it is important that you understand the relationship between them, as well as their differences.

Imagine your thought processes as being rather like a three-tier layer cake that would look a bit like this:

| |
|---|
| Day-to-day thoughts ('What an idiot I was to do that') |
| Assumptions (if this... then that...) |
| Basic beliefs (truths) |

## LINKING NEGATIVE THOUGHTS TO NEGATIVE BELIEFS

Negative thoughts are the 'top layer' of our thinking. They automatically pop in and out of our minds at the drop of a hat: 'Oh, I've messed up there'; 'I think I've just said the wrong thing'; 'I can tell he doesn't like me'; 'I'll never get this right'. In fact, these thoughts are your PFF in full throttle! For this reason, we tend to call them negative automatic thoughts (NATs) because the moment something happens, there they are. No reasoning, no pondering or internal debating: purely and simply the first thought that comes into our head.

Characteristics of negative automatic thoughts are:

▶ *they spring to mind without any effort*
▶ *they are event specific (e.g. something happens to cause us to think this way)*
▶ *they are easy to believe*
▶ *they can be difficult to stop*
▶ *they are unhelpful*
▶ *they keep your self-esteem low and make it difficult to change*
▶ *they are often not true.*

These NATs may be difficult to spot to start with, as you are probably not always aware that you have them (or you may define them as 'rational' thinking and see nothing negative about them), so the first step is to learn to recognize them.

Just becoming aware of these thoughts can help you begin to think in a more helpful, constructive way and with time develop positive automatic thoughts (PATs).

## Insight

We mistake *negative automatic* thinking for *rational* thinking. Learning to recognize self-defeating thoughts is the first step in eradicating them.

## Exercise

Write down what you consider to be negative characteristics about yourself. Presumably you consider these to be rational thoughts. Now see how many 'ticks' these thoughts get when you measure them against the characteristics of negative thoughts we have listed on page 33.

What might this mean about your thinking?

Negative beliefs are the 'bottom layer' of our thinking. We regard them as absolute; in our minds, they are not open to debate, as we (often erroneously) believe them to be facts. We have negative beliefs about:

- ▶ *ourselves ('I am worthless')*
- ▶ *others ('People always let you down')*
- ▶ *the world ('Crime is everywhere')*
- ▶ *the future ('Nothing will ever change').*

Negative beliefs can be so deep that we rarely even consider them or evaluate them; we simply accept their existence and build our other thought processes around them. We see them as absolute truths – 'Just the way things are' – *but they are very often wrong.*

Usually developing in our childhood, when we may not question what we learn, these negative or core beliefs can keep us trapped in our vicious cycle of low self-esteem.

## Anne's story

Anne's parents loved her very dearly, but decided that telling her that she could do even better – however high she achieved – would have a positive effect. However well Anne did, instead of being praised, she was told to 'Try even harder next time'. If she got 80% in a test, that was considered a failure and she must get 90% next time. If she got 90%, then only 100% was good enough. While Anne's parents felt that they were encouraging her to stretch herself and achieve more, unsurprisingly Anne developed a negative belief about herself along the lines of, 'No matter how hard I try, I'm just not good enough.'

Anne did get herself a good job. However, she was never able to fulfil her potential, since every time she started on a piece of challenging work, her 'I'm just not good enough' belief kicked in and she would think: 'I won't be able to do as good a job as they want. I'll get it wrong and everyone will see how incompetent I am. I'll let someone else take it on, and stick to simple tasks I can't mess up.'

Telling Anne to think more positively and that she will do a good job, won't help her at all – because it flies in the face of her basic belief that she isn't good enough.

You need to learn to identify unhelpful beliefs that prevent you from thinking more positively about yourself and your abilities, and to learn how to replace them with more realistic beliefs that will stop holding you back.

## Exercise

▶ *Consider any negative or core beliefs you might have about yourself. Write them down. Use the explanations on page 29 to ensure that they are basic beliefs.*
▶ *Ask yourself, at this moment, how strongly you believe each of them on a scale of 1 to 10 (where 1 = not much and 10 = absolutely).*

At the end of the book, you can re-rate them and see how much the strength of your beliefs has diminished.

## Rules for living

Negative assumptions link our beliefs to our day-to-day thinking. In this sense, they are the 'middle layer' of our thinking. They also become our rules for living, for example: if you hold a negative belief that you are a boring person, then you may make an assumption that 'If I talk to people socially, they will find me dull and uninteresting'. When you receive a party invitation, you may think 'I won't go. No one will want to talk to me.' Or you may go, but decide 'I'll just stand by myself in the corner and hope no one notices me. That way, I won't have to talk to people.'

You may develop a rule for living, such as 'I should not socialize', as you consider this will prevent your 'I am boring' belief being put to the test.

Anne, with her 'I'm not good enough' belief might hold an assumption that 'If I stay on the bottom rung of the career ladder, doing simple work I can easily handle, then hopefully I won't lose my job.'

Anne is developing a rule for living that it is better not to do anything that she finds difficult in order that her incompetence will never be discovered.

## Exercise

- ▶ *Can you identify any rules for living of your own? Look back at any basic beliefs that you managed to identify.*
- ▶ *Now ask yourself how you cope with these beliefs on a day-to-day basis. For example, if you believe you are unlikable, your rule for living might be to be as nice as pie to everyone at all times to mitigate against this.*
- ▶ *Write down three rules for living that you tend to use to help you overcome some of your self-defeating beliefs.*

The good news is that, as you gain in self-esteem and self acceptance, you will be able to consign these rules to the waste bin.

Remember, these thoughts, assumptions and beliefs are usually erroneous and it is not too hard to replace them with more helpful, accurate and positive alternatives.

## Insight
Becoming aware of the negative assumptions you make – and the rules for living you use as a result – are good first steps towards making positive changes.

# The role of emotion in low self-esteem

Having negative thoughts isn't actually what upsets us. It's the *emotions* that such thoughts trigger that cause us pain and distress. If you think you are a 'born loser' but the feeling that this generates for you is calm acceptance (unlikely, but bear with us for the sake of example), you will feel okay. If the feeling that this thought generates is total despair, then you will feel anything *but* okay.

Low self-esteem is problematic because it makes us *feel* badly about ourselves. Your thoughts generate these feelings. You *feel* the way you *think*.

At this point, you may well wish to argue the toss on this. You may still believe that the way you feel about yourself is due to external circumstances – other people failing to give you help and encouragement: poor parenting, lousy circumstances and 'bad breaks' that have caused reverses in your life.

## Workplace rebuff

Meet Peter. As he walks down a corridor to his office, he passes Jim. 'Hi Jim' says Peter, giving him a friendly wave. Jim walks on by and fails to acknowledge Peter at all.

If you were Peter, how would you feel?

- ▶ *Depressed ('Jim obviously doesn't like me.')*
- ▶ *Angry ('How rude. He couldn't even be bothered to say hello.')*
- ▶ *Amused ('Silly idiot – he must have forgotten his glasses.')*
- ▶ *Concerned ('He was obviously very preoccupied. I wonder if everything is okay?')*
- ▶ *Equable ('Oh well. Jim isn't always over-friendly.')*
- ▶ *Disappointed ('He didn't notice my new outfit.')*

To summarize: one event – two men passing in the corridor; five possible different thoughts about the event; five different feelings...

Why did we not finish the last sentence? Why did we not say 'Five different feelings about the event'?

Because the feelings were *not* generated by the event. The feelings were generated by the *thoughts* about the event.

**Insight**

Remember – how we feel is determined less by life events, and more by how we perceive those events.

## Exercise

Think through the following example of alternative possibilities.

*Jane is waiting in a restaurant for her girlfriend, Liz. They have not seen each other in several months and Jane is really looking forward to meeting up again. Then she gets a text from Liz to say she is held up at work and will be late. Jane waits on in vain – Liz doesn't turn up at all.*

Jot down how many different interpretations Jane could make of this event. See how many you can come up with.

### UNPACKING YOUR THOUGHTS AND FEELINGS

Does this idea now make more sense to you? This is an exceedingly important point as it is the foundation upon which you will create good self-esteem. It means that, instead of having to change all your life circumstances, you can work on changing your thinking – a much less daunting prospect – and this will change the way you feel.

Practise 'unpacking' your thoughts and your feelings. Use the table in the following exercise (make a few photocopies of the blank version on page 41 or copy it into your notebook). Look back over the last week and write down two or three events that have caused you to experience a reasonable level of emotion. Identify the emotion you felt and then write down what you were thinking at the time, or just before the event happened. Do you see more clearly how your thinking about the event largely determined how you felt about it?

## Exercise

Fill in at least three lines on the table today. Then fill in one each day for a week.

| The emotion you felt | The event that triggered this emotion | What you thought when this happened (self-critical thoughts generated by your PFF) | (leave empty for the moment) |
|---|---|---|---|
| (e.g. anxiety) | (e.g. client forgot important meeting) | (e.g. he isn't taking this seriously; he probably feels I'm not good enough to do the work he wants done) | |

Some people have trouble separating their thoughts and feelings. A simple tip is to remember that thoughts usually appear as sentences ('I hope I get this promotion') while feelings are almost always just one word: happy, sad, guilty, angry, cheerful, depressed, anxious, embarrassed and so on.

| The emotion you felt | The event that triggered this emotion | What you thought when this happened (self-critical thoughts generated by your PFF) | (leave empty for the moment) |
|---|---|---|---|
| | | | |

## Self-defeating behaviour

If someone with low self-esteem gets turned down for a job that they wanted very badly, their PFF may say to them: 'You're useless. You will never get a good job. There will always be other candidates far better than you.'

In this negative thinking state, what is this person's most likely behavioural response? The likelihood is that their *behaviour* will mirror their *thinking*. They may stop applying for jobs at all. They may set their sights lower, and apply for jobs well below their capabilities.

They may still continue to go for interviews but expect to do badly at them, which will be reflected in the impression they make, or fail to make.

In turn, this means that they are likely to remain unemployed – confirming that their negative thoughts and beliefs were correct. This will make the person feel emotionally low, and their self-esteem will sink even lower.

### Exercise

Look back the negative belief you noted on page 7.

▶ *Add the heading 'Self-defeating behaviour' and under that write down what you did as a result of your negative belief. (If you wrote 'I tackled the problem in a very positive way', then your self-esteem is not low, and you do not need this book!)*

## BRINGING IT ALL TOGETHER – DEVELOPING AN UNDERSTANDING OF THE PROBLEM

Let's now bring all these thoughts, feelings and behaviours together, so that we can develop a shared understanding of what maintains someone's low self-esteem. Look at the following diagram, which offers one possible explanation of the effects of the negative thinking that can accompany low self-esteem.

As you can see from the following diagram (in CBT terms, known as a 'conceptualization' or 'formulation'), thoughts, feelings and behaviour are all linked. This linking is what *maintains the problem* and keeps our self-esteem low.

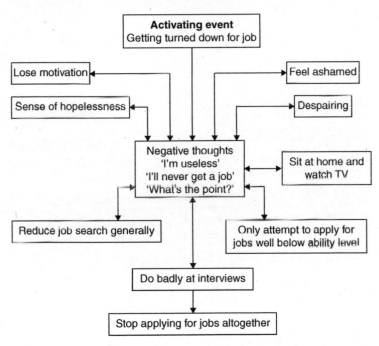

*Negative conceptualization*

Now look closely at the arrows. They have two points, both outwards, and then back inwards. Each negative emotion and action that you have in response to your negative thinking feeds back to you to reinforce your conviction that your negative views were correct. In other words, the emotions and actions driven *by* the thinking *maintain* the thinking. Look again at this formulation – there is absolutely nothing here that is going to break this cycle of despair and hopelessness. It is feeding in on itself and nothing changes; the sad fact is that the negative thoughts that are causing all this may be quite untrue.

The more we think negatively, the worse we feel, and the more negative our behaviour becomes. In turn, our negative behaviour causes us to feel even worse, and think even more pessimistically than we did before. Does this make sense?

The good news is that we can tap into any one of these areas, make a few small changes, and those changes will have a knock-on effect on the other areas. The following diagram will show you this.

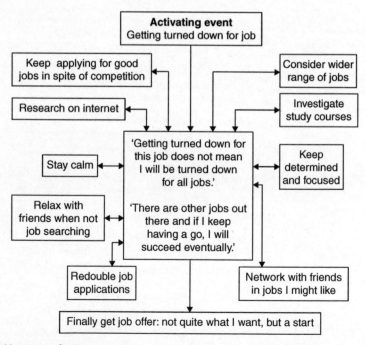

*Positive conceptualization*

44

Can you see what is going on here? Look at the two formulations. The event was the same. Yet the event created thoughts which drove both emotional responses and actions that either maintained and consolidated the problem, or drove a way forward out of the problem. If you can appreciate and understand the importance of this, you will be well on the way to improving your own self-esteem immeasurably.

## Insight

Negative thoughts and emotions trigger negative behaviours. We are often not aware that these behaviours are self-defeating. Changing any one aspect – thinking, feelings, behaviours – will change the others.

## Exercise

While this may seem hard at first, we would like you to attempt a formulation of your own that may help to explain the maintenance of a particular problem that you have.

▶ *Simply follow the examples on pages 43 and 44 and – using the most recent example of an event that caused you some upset – first write down centrally what your thoughts were.*
▶ *Then write down how you felt and acted as a result of these thoughts.*
▶ *Now look at what you have written. Did these thoughts, feelings and actions resolve your problem, or did they maintain it?*

Understanding where we may be going wrong is an essential first step, as is appreciating the basic relationship between thoughts, feelings, actions and outcomes. Now we need to move further forward and start to enable you to make the changes that will defeat your low self-esteem and replace it with a strong and healthily balanced view of yourself.

---

## Replacing self-defeating thoughts and beliefs

*There are no impossible dreams, just our limited perceptions of what is possible.*

Beth Mende Conny

You have now learned to identify your self-defeating thoughts, and the emotions and behaviour patterns that go with them. However, up to now, your PFF has had the upper hand.

Now is the time to give your PFF a great big kick out of the door. Remind yourself strongly... that how you feel is based on what you think. If you want to feel good about yourself, you need to think realistically, not negatively.

### USING A THOUGHT RECORD

The best way to challenge your PFF is by writing down your negative thoughts and emotions, and then writing down more positive or realistic alternatives. This is called a thought record, since although you are recording what has happened, the main focus is on what you *thought* about what happened. The more you practise filling in a thought record, the easier it becomes to spot these thoughts – and to understand the effect they have on how you feel.

You have already begun getting used to writing down your thoughts, with the simple record that you tried out earlier in this chapter. Now you are ready to move on to more comprehensive negative thought challenging.

**First, write it down**

Writing things down can be a chore: 'It takes so much time'; 'I can never find a pen'; 'Can't I just do this in my head?'

No – sorry! Writing things down is far more powerful than simply trying to think the situation through. It causes you to really think hard, and all the time you are writing, you are thinking. Take a look at the thought record on next page. You will see that it is an extension of the record you have already filled in. This format will change again (for the last time) a little later in the book, so just make one or two photocopies for the moment to use until then or copy it into your notebook.

## Insight
Simply having an awareness of negative thinking (rather than assuming that it is rational thinking) can help us feel better.

## Exercise

Copy out the thought record on the next page – or take a photocopy if you can.

▶ Practise filling it in, working across the page.
▶ Fill in each column for at least one negative thought.

Don't worry if it does not come too easily yet. This is just a start, and we will continue to give you further tips and ideas to turn this into a really useful tool.

A thought record

| Date and time, and what happened | What you thought when this event happened (How strongly do you believe this on a scale from 1 to 10?) | How you felt (How strongly did you feel this on a scale from 1 to 10?) | Alternative thoughts (Generate at least two or three alternatives. Rate your belief in them on a scale from 1 to 10) | How do you feel now? (Rate any possible change, now you have looked at things more positively) |
|---|---|---|---|---|
| | | | | |

# TIPS FOR FILLING IN YOUR THOUGHT RECORD

## Finding alternative responses

You may initially find it hard to come up with alternative responses. This is because your natural tendency is to be self-critical – and to believe these self-critical thoughts to be true.

## Rating your thoughts and emotions

You will notice we ask you to rate (subjectively) how strongly you believe your negative thoughts, the intensity of your emotion, and the strength of your belief in the alternative responses. This is so that you can check that you have picked the thought that generates the emotion.

For example, if your negative thought is 'I am overdressed for this function' and your emotion is 80% panic, you may not have logged the right thought.

Ask yourself *why* being overdressed is causing you such anxiety and you will get closer to your real concern. The answer might be 'I will look completely out of place and everyone will laugh at me.'

*Now* you have identified the thought which might cause such panic.

This is an important point, as your thought record will not help you unless you are working with what really bothers you. So do take some time to consider what is *really* upsetting you.

## Be firm!

Be very firm with your rebuttals; really challenge and talk back to your PFF. Come up with at least two or three alternatives, not just one. There are always several different ways of looking at the same thing. Find them.

You may initially find that, although you come up with alternative thoughts, you don't really believe them. You still believe your self-critical thoughts more strongly as you have had years of self-indoctrination. This will gradually change – and you will learn further skills in later steps to help you to reinforce your beliefs in a more positive outlook.

Rating the strength of your emotions at the end of the thought record checks whether challenging the negative thoughts does in fact help you to feel better.

Once you are familiar with identifying negative thoughts, you can examine how unrealistic or unhelpful they are and whether they are useful to you. Studies have shown that doing this can improve your mood and make you feel more in control of your situation and your life.

### Insight

Challenging your self-defeating thoughts is a very powerful way of loosening the grip they have on your self-esteem. Be sure to rebut these thoughts very strongly.

### Exercise

Begin using your thought record on a daily basis. Set yourself a goal of challenging one negative thought each day for the next two weeks. As you get more used to doing this, you will eventually no longer need to write your thoughts down, but please ensure you do so initially.

Now that you are used to using a thought record – and used to the idea that to improve your self-esteem it is vital to challenge your existing ways of thinking and acting and to replace them with alternative ideas about yourself that will raise your spirits and make you feel a great deal more confident and accepting – we want to help you to develop a variety of skills and techniques in order to do this. A basic and simple thought record is a start – but only a start. So let's look in further detail at how we can get rid of your PFF through a variety of excellent techniques.

# Recognizing distorted thinking patterns

We cannot emphasize this enough: the feelings generated by low self-esteem such as depression and anxiety to name but a few, are caused by *distorted* thinking. Once you learn to challenge these thoughts, you will immediately change how you feel – both about yourself and life in general.

Recognizing distorted thinking is not always easy. We assume that all our thinking is rational and 'correct'. In a good frame of mind, it may be (though not always). But when we are in a poor frame of mind, our thinking can become negative and distorted without our realizing that this is happening.

## COMPOUNDING OUR THINKING ERRORS

The problem is that, once we start making thinking errors, we tend to 'stick with them'. They become – as we have learned already – assumptions and beliefs that we retain unless we make an effort to recognize them and change them.

Psychologists have identified a number of common thinking errors that most of us make some of the time (and some of us make all of the time). If you know what these are, and recognize them, it will make your challenging rebuttals much easier to formulate. Read through them and place a tick against any you feel apply to you. Here is the first...

### Generalizing the specific
You come to a *general* conclusion based on a *single* incident or piece of evidence. If you have a minor car accident, you decide you are a dangerous driver (and must never drive again). One failed recipe means you cannot cook and wobbly stitching means you cannot sew. Someone treats you unfairly and you say, 'Nobody likes me'. You use words such as 'always' and 'never', 'nobody' and 'everyone' to make a general rule out of a specific situation.

When you challenge your thinking, ask yourself if you are taking a specific situation and making a general assumption about it. Be sure to turn this back to specific thinking. For example, if you make a mistake, don't tell yourself that you are hopeless, tell yourself that you did not do *that specific thing* as well as usual. If you get rejected, don't tell yourself that you are unlovable, tell yourself that *this particular person* was not right for you.

> ### Insight
> Feelings generated by low self-esteem – such as depression and anxiety to name but a few – are caused by *distorted*, rather than rational thinking.

## Exercise

We all use distorted thinking patterns at times. It is very common indeed. With that thought in mind, look at what you have already written in your thought record.

▶ *Have you made any generalizations about yourself or your behaviour?*
▶ *If so, be sure to come up with an alternative thought that is* specific.

Here are some further common thinking errors to add to your thinking skills base.

### Mind reading
Mind reading is one of the commonest thinking errors we make when our self-esteem is low. Without their saying so, we 'know' what people are thinking and why they act the way their do. In particular, we are able to divine how people are feeling towards us.

It is fatal to self-esteem because we think that everyone agrees with our negative opinions of ourselves, for example:

- ▶ *'I know he thinks I am boring.'*
- ▶ *'I can tell she doesn't like me.'*
- ▶ *'I'm sure they don't really want me in their group.'*

Yet we are jumping to conclusions without any real evidence – and, for some reason, we only seem to have the gift of mind reading *negative* views. Interestingly, we seldom seem to develop a talent for mind reading positive thoughts!

Writing such thoughts down in a thought record will help you to re-evaluate this supernatural thinking ability and challenge your mind reading certainties.

## Filtering

We take the negative details from a situation and then magnify them, while at the same time filtering out all the positive aspects, for example:

> *You have dressed beautifully for a formal evening and your partner pays you the well-deserved compliment of saying how nice you look. However, as you leave the room he mentions that the hem of your skirt is not quite straight at the back. You now feel that you no longer look lovely, and that the evening will be spoiled while you worry about the hem of your dress. The fact that, apart from this, you look stunning quite passes you by.*

## Polarized thinking

We think of people, situations or events in extremes such as good or bad: 'I must be perfect or I am a failure'; 'If I'm not beautiful, I'm ugly'. There is no middle ground. The problem is that we usually find ourselves on the negative end of our polarized extremes. So if we cannot be perfect, we must be all bad. If we don't get the job you want, our future is ruined. If our relationship doesn't work out, we will never find true love.

## Catastrophizing

We expect disaster. We notice or hear about a problem, and start on the 'What ifs?', for example:

- ▶ *'What if tragedy strikes?'*
- ▶ *'What if it happens to me?'*

We then decide that if this terrible thing did happen to us, we would not be able to cope.

## Personalization

This involves thinking that everything people do or say is some kind of reaction to us.

Perhaps your partner mentions that the home is looking a little untidy. You will immediately 'read' this comment as a criticism of your housekeeping skills. Or maybe someone mentions that your work team haven't achieved their targets this month. You instantly decide that this comment is really directed at you personally.

You find yourself becoming unnecessarily defensive and possibly even causing ill-feeling if you take someone's passing remark as personal criticism.

## Blaming

This is the opposite of personalization. We hold other people, organizations or even the universe responsible for our problems, for example:

- ▶ *'She has made me feel terrible.'*
- ▶ *'That company ruined my life.'*
- ▶ *'Life is so unfair.'*

We feel unable to change our views or our circumstances, as we see ourselves as victims of other people's thoughtlessness and meanness.

## It's all my fault

Instead of feeling a victim, we feel responsible for the pain and happiness of everyone around us.

If your daughter misses a lift taking her to a special occasion, you feel totally to blame for not having chivvied her along (even though she is 17 and has taken the whole afternoon getting ready). Or if your firm loses an important client, you will find a way to believe that something you did caused this.

**Fallacy of fairness**
We feel resentful because we think we know what's fair, but other people won't agree with us. We continually attempt to prove that our opinions and actions are correct. We expect other people to change their views and actions if we pressure or cajole them enough. We try to change people in this way when we believe our hopes for happiness depend entirely on their behaving differently.

**Insight**
While it can be hard to discover that much of your thinking is biased by negative distortions, acknowledging this is the first step to change. The next step is to use this knowledge to help you with your self-esteem.

## Exercise

▶ *Show the list of thinking errors on pages 51 to 55 to friends, family and/or work colleagues, and ask them if they recognize any that they use themselves. (In all probability, they will smile wryly as they admit to most of them!)*
▶ *How do you feel, knowing that these are errors most of us make?*
▶ *Now look through your thought record and see if there is one thinking error that you use more than others. Which one?*

Checking out possible thinking errors is another excellent skill to add to your toolbox. Make sure that you use it regularly.

# More tools to help you challenge self-defeating thoughts

### Checking for evidence

What goes through you mind when you challenge your PFF and write down more positive, rational alternatives? Many people write diligently, but the thought in their mind is, 'I don't really believe this – what I really still believe are the views of my PFF.'

How can you strengthen your belief in your alternative views? There is one extremely helpful tool – thought by many to be the most important 'thought shifter' around – and that is to ask a simple question: 'If this is really so, where's the evidence?'

## Jenny's story

Jenny was concerned about her job. She had heard about the possibility of redundancies at her firm and she started thinking about her own performance and whether her boss might find a reason to get rid of her. The more she thought about it, the more weaknesses she came up with: being late for an important meeting last week, failing to sign up a new client company that had looked promising – was she losing her grip?

Over lunch with a colleague, Anne, Jenny voiced her concerns. Her friend of course asked Jenny why she was coming to this negative conclusion, and Jenny cited what had happened – her 'evidence' for her pessimistic thinking. Anne expressed surprise: 'But Jenny, several people were late for that meeting due to the tube strike – it couldn't be helped. And while it was disappointing to lose the client, it may not have been your fault at all – you made an excellent presentation, and there were many possible reasons why the client may not have gone ahead. Now think of all the new business you *have* brought in to the firm this year, which you seem to be discounting.' In essence, Anne was presenting Jenny with evidence to contradict Jenny's self-defeating thoughts. But Jenny had not thought of this herself, as she was too focused on her negative views of her abilities.

This is what can happen to us when our self-esteem is low. We focus on the negative and ignore the helpful evidence. So we want you to introduce this element into your thought record. You will learn how to do this in the next step.

**Insight**

Always ask yourself 'What evidence do I have?' Having to provide this will help you move towards better-balanced thinking, and to believe it more strongly.

## Exercise: giving evidence in your thought record

Practise this skill. Look back to your most recent self-critical thought.

▶ *Ask yourself what evidence you had to support it. If you were a barrister in a court of law, could you provide evidence against it? What would you say?*
▶ *Look at the full version of your thought record on page 59. You will see that there are now two extra columns. The first asks you to find evidence to support your PFF's negative comments. For example, if you have looked in the mirror just before going out and thought 'I look dreadful', where is your evidence?*
    ▷ *Is your hair a mess? (fix it)*
    ▷ *Are your clothes wrong? (change them)*
    ▷ *Or do you simply feel low about yourself?*
▶ *Start looking for the evidence to support your self-critical thoughts. You will usually find it harder than you think to come up with solid reasoning. Would the response 'Oh, I just do' stand up in a court of law? What would a judge think of your evidence? Would the judge accept it or throw it out?*

*(Contd)*

▶ The second new column asks you to find evidence for your alternative thinking. Using the example from this exercise, an alternative thought might be, 'I really don't look too bad'. It will be easier to believe this if you write evidence that might be along the lines of:
  ▷ 'My partner always tells me I look nice when I get dressed up.'
  ▷ And/or 'My best friend has asked to borrow this dress next Saturday.'
▶ As you get used to finding evidence for your thinking, it will loosen your PFF's hold on your mind through tangible, logical argument, rather than simply repeating optimistic alternatives that you don't really feel hold water. This is a very powerful skill.
▶ Make several copies of the blank thought record on page 60. It is now a very important tool for you. Use it every time your self-esteem plummets, from now until you begin to find that you automatically challenge your thinking without having to write it down.

Full thought record

| Date and time, and what happened | What you thought when this event happened (How strongly do you believe this on a scale from 1 to 10?) | How you felt (How strongly did you feel this on a scale from 1 to 10?) | Evidence to support your negative thought | Alternative thoughts (Generate at least two or three alternatives. Rate your belief in them from 1 to 10) | Evidence to support your alternative thoughts | How do you feel now? (Rate any possible change, now you have looked at things a little more positively) |
|---|---|---|---|---|---|---|
| Failed driving test | I'll never learn to drive (generalization) (8) | Depressed (8) | After ten lessons, I could not pass. | This does not mean I will never pass. (6) Many people fail their test first time. (6). | My instructor has been very complimentary. My brother failed his test twice and then passed. | A little more optimistic. I will book another test. (9) |

Full thought record

| Date and time, and what happened | What you thought when this event happened (How strongly do you believe this on a scale from 1 to 10?) | How you felt (How strongly did you feel this on a scale from 1 to 10?) | Evidence to support your negative thought | Alternative thoughts (Generate at least two or three alternatives. Rate your belief in them from 1 to 10) | Evidence to support your alternative thoughts | How do you feel now? (Rate any possible change, now you have looked at things a little more positively) |
|---|---|---|---|---|---|---|
| | | | | | | |

## ARE YOU GUILTY OF 'THE TYRANNY OF THE 'SHOULDS'?

*When we are capable of living in the moment free from the tyranny of 'shoulds', we will have peaceful hearts.*

Joan Borysenko

### Shoulds, musts and oughts

A great deal of negative, self-defeating thinking comes from using the words 'should', 'must' and 'ought'. These words imply personal failure almost every time we use them. They cause us to make demands on ourselves, and suggest that we cannot meet those demands, for example:

▶ *'I should have known better.'*
▶ *'I should be able to achieve this.'*
▶ *'I shouldn't have done that.'*

This is not positive thinking. We think this is positive self-talk – that we are motivating ourselves by telling ourselves these things. In fact, the exact opposite happens: 'I must be such and such (polite, charming, clever and so on)... and since I am not, I then feel badly about myself.'

And it's not only us. When our self-esteem is low, and we feel sorry for ourselves, these 'shoulds', 'musts' and 'oughts' extend to others. People 'should' be nicer to us. Others 'must' consider us when making their plans. Colleagues 'ought' to take into account how busy we are before dumping extra work on our desk.

We would like you to visualize yourself gathering all of these words up, and dropping them into the nearest rubbish bin.

What can you put in their place? One option is using acceptance; adopting the idea that it is okay to be fallible ourselves and that others also make mistakes.

You can also replace 'shoulds', 'must's and 'oughts', with softer, less absolute and critical language, for example: 'It would be great if I can achieve this, but it's not the end of the world if I don't'; 'It would have been better if I'd remembered to… but I am as fallible as the next person.'

Give this a go. Write down three sentences using 'should', 'must' or 'ought' in a way that relates to negative thoughts that you have/had about yourself in a recent situation. Then write the sentences again, having binned the 'shoulds', 'musts' and 'oughts'.

Did you find that easy, or difficult? You now need to practise this a great deal. You will find that your confidence will improve as you stop being quite so hard on yourself (and others).

> **Insight**
> Put all your inappropriate and stress-inducing 'shoulds', 'musts' and 'oughts' in the rubbish bin – forever!

## Exercise

Focus on how often you use the word 'should', and replace it with a softer option. This will increase your awareness of this thinking error, and encourage you to make the change permanent.

### CONFIDENCE-BUILDING TECHNIQUE: 'ASK A FRIEND'

Many of us have a tendency to be far harder on ourselves than on others. We make allowances for the mistakes of friends and work colleagues, we understand, for others, that a 'bad step' doesn't make a 'bad person' – yet when it comes to ourselves, we show ourselves no leniency.

An excellent tool for helping ourselves to be more self-accepting is this. Ask yourself the following question:

> *'If my best friend was feeling this way, rather than me, what would I say to them? What evidence would I point out to them to help them see that their pessimistic thoughts or negative self-assessment was not 100% true?'*

The answer you will probably come up with will usually be quite different to your own, negative self-talk. We are always so much wiser and more constructive at finding positive qualities in others than we are in ourselves. Use your evidence-gathering skills to prove your point, and you will probably find how little evidence there is for the self-defeating thoughts that your 'friend' has.

Another good question to ask yourself is:

> *'Would my best friend agree with my negative views of myself? If not, what might they say about me?'*

Most importantly, then ask yourself,

> *'Why would my friend see me differently to the way I see myself?'*

Become your own 'best friend'. Use the questions above regularly, and you will find that it will really help to see yourself and your situation in a more positive way.

## Insight

Always advise yourself as though you are advising your best friend. It is the most useful skill.

▶ *Pick three negative aspects of yourself, or events where you feel that you did not come up to scratch (as you consider it). Jot them down in your notebook.*

▶ *Now imagine that your best friend is describing these worries to you. Write down exactly what you would tell them.*

▶ *Does this give you a new perspective on your views about yourself?*

We spent some time earlier in this chapter helping you to understand more about personal beliefs, and how they can almost 'slip by unnoticed' when we make observations about ourselves. As we have explained, this is because we tend not to question their validity. Now you need to start doing this.

## Tackling negative beliefs

You may find it hard to move away from pessimistic thinking if your negative beliefs are deeply entrenched. However, you can still learn to replace these beliefs with a more compassionate and positive view of yourself.

Remember that while our day-to-day self-critical thoughts tend to evolve due to specific events, beliefs we hold about ourselves are absolute. For example: 'I am boring', 'I am hopeless' or 'I am unlikable'.

Can you identify any beliefs you may have about yourself that contribute to your low self-esteem? If you found that difficult, try this: think back to early experiences that encouraged you to think badly about yourself. What conclusions did you come to about yourself based on events in your childhood?

Think about the things you may do to keep yourself 'safe', for example: 'I don't socialize much'. Why not? Your answer may help you to discover a belief, for example: 'I am boring' or 'I can't talk to people'.

Look back at the work you are doing with your thought record. Do you notice any repeating patterns for the critical way(s) you describe yourself? What negative beliefs about yourself do your negative thoughts reflect?

Where you remain unsure as to what is really going on for you, here is another excellent technique to use.

## THE 'DOWNWARD ARROW' TECHNIQUE

Take any thought from your thought record, and apply a downward arrow to it in the following way.

In the example on the next page, you are worried about a party you have accepted to go to, and are beginning to feel very nervous.

Using this skill, you have uncovered a core belief (two, in fact) that you have about yourself and which you can now work on.

You can also ask yourself another question: 'What is the personal meaning to me if this does or doesn't occur?'

Your answer might be: 'I am totally unlikable.'

Does this make sense to you, as a useful, probing technique? Practise it a great deal – it is actually a vital component in ensuring that you are working on the 'causal' thought or belief (this is simply the thought or belief that is truly responsible for how you are feeling) and not on some superficial idea that won't be relevant to helping you feel better.

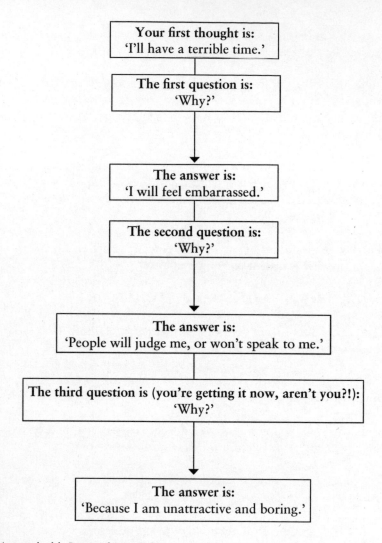

*An example of the Downward Arrow Technique*

Once you have identified any basic, self-critical beliefs, you can begin to start chipping away at them, and replacing them with more helpful and realistic, positive beliefs. In this way, your self-esteem and self-acceptance will increase greatly.

## Exercise

Use the suggestions we have made above to continue to look at self-critical beliefs you may have about yourself.

Especially look for beliefs that you have held for a long time.

If these beliefs stem from childhood, recall any particular words of criticism that you may have absorbed.

### STRATEGIES FOR REPLACING OLD BELIEFS WITH NEW ONES

*Success seems to be largely a matter of hanging on after others have let go.*

William Feather

Start by focusing on your strengths and good points. Revisit page 22 where we asked you to list ten personal qualities. We would now like you to add a further ten. You will need to refer back to them, so keep them by you.

You may find this next step difficult – but it is not impossible. We are asking you now to write down your smallest achievements, abilities and personal qualities. We want you to get used to focusing on your *strengths* rather than your *weaknesses*. This is not something you will normally do, so it will not come naturally or easily – all the more reason for doing it! For example:

*Look at your working days. Whether you are home-based or office-based, there will be plenty of examples on a daily basis of things you are quite good at (perhaps typing, cooking, keeping things neat, staying calm when others are getting worked up). Once you start thinking over the last week, you should not find it difficult.*

## DON'T RATE YOURSELF

Incorporate things you may like about yourself – 'I am kind', 'I am patient' – as well as things you can do. Don't rate your abilities and qualities. You don't have to be the best at anything before you write it down. Even being quite modest at something counts as a positive: 'I don't get too worked up when people are late' or 'I managed to stick to my diet for a week' all count.

### REFOCUS

One of the goals of this exercise is to get you to focus differently. Remember what you have learned – it is not who you are or what happened – it is your *perceptions* of who you are or what happened that define your thinking and your self-esteem. You are now learning to shift your perceptions from negative to positive.

What you have *also* achieved is to collect a body of evidence to help you ditch your self-critical beliefs. Keep this evidence with you and move on to the next step.

## Insight
Focusing on what you like about yourself and what you do well will help you start to see yourself differently.

### BRINGING POSITIVE QUALITIES INTO FOCUS WITH A POSITIVE DATA LOG

A positive data log (PDL) is an excellent tool for getting you to question self-critical beliefs. It is simple, but very effective. Take a negative belief that you hold, and – to start with – find any evidence that you can that might suggest your belief is not true all the time.

You can use some of the evidence that you collected previously.
Use the chart on the next page. An example might be:

**Self-critical belief:** *I am unlikable.*
**New, alternative belief:** *I am quite likable.*
**Evidence to support your new belief and weaken your old belief:**
*I do have a few friends.*
*I have been invited to several social occasions so far this year.*
*In general, people are pleasant to me.*
*My work colleagues are friendly.*
*I get invited to workplace social functions.*
*I do my best to be kind and thoughtful.*
*My neighbour thanked me for my helpfulness*
*I normally have a steady partner and I have been in two long-term*
*    relationships.*
*Although I said 'No', I have had a marriage proposal.*
*I am close to my family.*

We have not suggested too big a swing from negative belief to
positive belief. Changing beliefs can take several months, so a
'middle of the road' alternative will serve you better than to start
with than an unrealistic, 'I am totally likable'. Now give this a go
for yourself.

## Exercise

Start filling in your positive data log. We suggest you make
up two or three, and gradually add to your evidence for
each one over a period of a week or two, as you observe
events and experiences that support them.

*(Contd)*

## Positive data log

Self-critical belief: _____

New, alternative belief: _____

Evidence to support your new belief and weaken your old belief

1 _____
2 _____
3 _____
4 _____
5 _____
6 _____
7 _____
8 _____
9 _____
10 _____
11 _____
12 _____
13 _____
14 _____
15 _____
16 _____
17 _____
18 _____
19 _____
20 _____

Measure the improving strength of your new beliefs by rating them. Self-critical beliefs take longer to change than our day-to-day, event-specific negative thinking. This is, as you have already learned, because they have been around a lot longer and are more absolute.

However, you will begin to see some change fairly quickly and you will gain encouragement from using a rating scale to track this. Don't go for 100% – it's unrealistic and unattractive!

You do not need to see an absolute (100%) gain. That would be both difficult to achieve and undesirable. For example: if your original, self-critical belief was, 'I am unlikable' and the belief you would like to replace it with is, 'I am likable most of the time' (note we are not striving for a total opposite, but a realistic alternative) then your rating scale might look like this:

Desired belief: 'I am likable most of the time.'

Initial strength of that belief: (place a X over the percentage)

X
0%       25%       50%       75%       100%

Desired belief: 'I am likable most of the time.'

Strength of belief after two weeks of skills practice:

                         X
0%       25%       50%       75%       100%

Of course, these are subjective ratings, but you will have a very good 'feel' for how you are progressing, and by continuing to use your thought record and positive data log, you will find that you are gathering more and more evidence to support your new beliefs. You are training your mind to refocus on your more positive characteristics, and to re-evaluate the accuracy of your negative beliefs.

## Insight

Be patient as you work for change. Don't expect overnight success and then give up because of lack of it. Rating any changes is a very helpful way of seeing some improvement – even if it is only slight, it is a success.

Rate your self-critical beliefs as you see them now. You may find that, immediately, you don't really want to put your X over 0%. Place it on the scale as accurately as you can.

What does the fact that not all your crosses are on zero tell you about your thinking?

## TESTING NEGATIVE PREDICTIONS

Here is a further skill for challenging negative thoughts and beliefs. You can use simple, practical experiments to test out negative predictions, for example: Mary believed that she was dull and uninteresting. What sort of assumptions or rules for living do you think Mary might have? Perhaps:

- ▶ *'If I speak to people they will find out how dull and boring I am.' (assumption) and*
- ▶ *'If I keep myself to myself, people won't realize how hopeless I am.' (rule for living)*

Mary was asked to devise some experiments to test out her beliefs, and she came up with the following.

### Experiment one
*Make a simple comment to at least ten people – who could include shop assistants, receptionists, the milkman, and so on.*
**Mary's prediction:** *'No one will speak to me. They will think I am odd and I will feel embarrassed.'*
**What actually happened:** *Six people began a conversation with Mary. Three people smiled at her. One person ignored her comments.*

## Experiment two

*Invite a friend to visit the theatre or cinema with you.*

**Mary's prediction:** *'Whoever I ask will make an excuse and I will feel unlikable.'*

**What actually happened:** *The first person Mary asked could not come but sounded genuinely disappointed. The second person accepted immediately and thanked Mary for thinking of her.*

## Experiment three

*At lunch in the staff canteen, ask to sit with different people each day for a week, and note their responses.*

**Mary's prediction:** *'This will be embarrassing. People will find it hard to say "No" and I will feel I'm intruding.'*

**What actually happened:** *On one of the days, the person she asked said they were just leaving the table, and on another, the colleagues she chose were engrossed in a work problem and Mary was unable to join in. However, on three of the five days, Mary's colleagues welcomed her and chatted to her with interest. Mary relaxed and actually enjoyed it.*

Testing out her negative beliefs encouraged Mary to modify her 'I'm dull and boring' belief to one of, 'Some people find me quite interesting'.

Mary was also able to use her experiments to add to her positive data log. If Mary continues with her experiments, she may be able to modify this belief even further, perhaps to 'I appear interesting to most people'.

## Insight

Testing out negative predictions is an excellent way to dispute negative beliefs. The worst that can happen is that it is as bad as you predict, and the likelihood is you will learn that what actually happens is quite different to your negative expectations.

Devise a small experiment for yourself to test out one of your self-critical beliefs. Make it very simple and easy, so that you are not tempted to duck out. Make a prediction, and measure it against what actually happens.

## Bringing your positive qualities into focus

Many people suggest that the simple way to get rid of our PFF is simply to 'think positively'. This is not entirely without merit. It is, however, very difficult to do – or we would all feel remarkably good about ourselves all the time, which is not the case.

So how can we structure 'think positively' to give it more opportunity as a concept to help us? How do we keep our positive qualities in the forefront of our minds? American psychologist, Professor Martin Seligman, has come up with an exercise he calls 'The Three Blessings'. We are adjusting it slightly for the purposes of this book, and would like to rename it 'Bringing your positive qualities into focus'. Professor Seligman has undertaken wide-scale research in the United States that shows, empirically, that doing this exercise for as little as one week has a very positive effect on our view of ourselves and life generally.

You may question its simplicity, but we would ask you to consider for a moment why it is so effective.

You are simply asked, at the end of each day, to write down three positive things that have happened that have been caused by a positive quality of your own. The events may be very insignificant, for example: 'The post person smiled at me on my way out.'

However, the key to this – and the harder thing to do – is to then explain why it happened in terms of any positive aspect of yourself, for example: 'The post person smiled at me... because I appeared friendly.'

One or two other examples to help you get the idea might be:

▶ *'I brought my work colleague a cup of coffee.' Relating this to a personal quality, you might say: 'I am a thoughtful person, at least some of the time.'*
▶ *'I managed to plumb in the dishwasher'... 'I do have some DIY skills.'*

Don't be over-modest in your assessments. If you have done anything reasonably okay, allow yourself to feel good about it. Feeling good about yourself is not a crime!

## Exercise

▶ *Fill in the chart on the next page for a week at least. Evaluate any changes in your thinking.*
▶ *Ask yourself why this might be making a difference and what you see as the main purpose of this exercise.*

**Insight**
Don't dismiss this simple exercise too lightly. It has proven to be very effective.

This has been a long, but very important early chapter for you, as the skills it contains set the foundation for everything else that you now do.

**Bringing my positive qualities into focus**

| Date | What happened/what did I do? (three events) | What does this say about me that is positive? |
|------|---------------------------------------------|-----------------------------------------------|
|      |                                             |                                               |

# 10 THINGS TO REMEMBER

1 *Your low self-esteem comes far less from terrible events in your life, and far more from unhelpful, negative thinking about those events.*

2 *Make sure you hold in your mind the difference between beliefs and facts.*

3 *We hold the beliefs at the 'bottom' layer of our thinking. They seem like 'truths' to us, and because of this they form the assumptions we make.*

4 *Thoughts alone are not enough to cause low self-esteem – it is the emotions that the thoughts engender that can cause us pain and distress.*

5 *Negative automatic thoughts, assumptions and beliefs encourage us to behave in a self-defeating way and turn events into self-fulfilling prophecies.*

6 *It is vitally important to keep records of your thoughts, feelings and behaviours and use these to search for new ways of looking at yourself or life events.*

7 *The sense of failure that 'should', 'must' and 'ought' can induce when you don't achieve what they demand will reduce your confidence and self-belief and damage your self-esteem.*

8 *Identifying unhelpful beliefs is just the first, albeit vital, step to change and build up confidence: now you need to start using your skills and resources to change them.*

*(Contd)*

**9** *Once you are accustomed to modifying your thoughts cognitively (for example, simply by thinking about them differently), you need to start testing new ideas.*

**10** *A proven, valuable tool for success is to write down three positive things that happen to you each day, coupled with a brief explanation of why those things might have happened.*

# 3

................................

# The perfection trap

In this chapter you will learn:
- *how perfectionism lowers self-esteem, rather than raising it*
- *how perfectionist views develop*
- *to look for thinking errors that maintain your perfectionism*
- *to shake off perfectionist thinking that is based on outdated influences*
- *that feeling good about yourself is not always based on perfect performance.*

## What is perfectionism?

Many people's low self-esteem is driven by unhelpful thinking about the standards they should be able to reach in order to feel good about themselves.

Are you one of these people? Many clients we work with are. A commonality is that they are often bright and intelligent, and are usually doing exceedingly well in life. Yet their self-esteem remains low, because they are still not reaching the perfect way of being they believe they should attain.

## PERFECTIONISM = SETTING YOURSELF UP FOR FAILURE

This is because it is almost impossible to get a perfect score in life. In many cases, it is impossible to even know what a 'perfect score' would be, for example:

> ▶ *Is there a cast iron, concrete definition for perfect beauty?*
> ▶ *Is there one for being a perfect pianist... or mathematician?*
> ▶ *What about a perfect parent?*

How would you even know if you had reached perfection? Even being the best in the world at something doesn't mean that you are perfect at it.

So by trying to be perfect, you will almost certainly fail every time.

How is this likely to affect your self-esteem? The answer, for most people, is hugely. It means that, no matter how well you do, you are never able to see yourself as the success you would like to be. It also means that you may spend so much time – over and above what others would consider normal – on individual tasks and targets that you then fall behind in other areas, and this also weakens your ability to see yourself as anything other than someone who is failing all round.

## WHERE DOES PERFECTIONISM COME FROM?

Experience shows us that perfectionism usually develops in childhood, probably from parents who drive a child to constantly do better; 80% should be 90%, 90% should be 100%. Being in the football team isn't good enough unless you are Captain. Playing an instrument requires you to practise relentlessly and then some more. This does not mean that the parents are unloving, but rather, they feel that by constantly moving the goalposts their children will try harder and achieve more. The legacy for many young people is they feel that, no matter what they do, it is never good enough.

We may carry this feeling with us into adulthood as a self-defeating belief, and – even though we are probably very successful in most areas of our lives – we will constantly criticize ourselves and feel worthless because we aren't getting things perfect.

## Insight

Perfection is impossible to quantify, and therefore all in your mind. Don't see yourself as a failure, but someone who is very able, just setting the bar too high.

### YOU CAN CHANGE

Change is not too hard – and it is important. You are probably someone who could have very high self-esteem, so don't waste it! You can learn to see yourself and the world differently and feel more confident... read on to discover how.

## Insight

It is always worth weighing up the pros and cons of your thinking styles, to see if there is a more helpful way to look at things.

## Exercise

If perfectionism is a problem for you, list the areas in which you feel you need to be perfect. On the basis that, for you perfection = 100%, rate how close you are to that for each of the areas you have listed. Now think of two friends or work colleagues, and rate what you consider to be their abilities in these same areas. If you have rated them lower than yourself (or the same):

▶ *Are they as anxious about it as you are?*
▶ *Do they mind as much? If not, why not?*

*(Contd)*

How can you shift this thinking?

First, write down three beliefs you have about striving for perfection. For example:

▶ *'I must always try to be perfect.'*
▶ *'Anything less than complete success is failure.'*
▶ *'Others will think less of me if I make mistakes.'*
▶ *'I cannot live with myself if I let my standards slip.'*

Using the chart on the next page, take each attitude in turn and write down what you see as the advantages, to you, of holding this view. On the other side of the chart, write down any disadvantages to you of holding this view. For any views where the disadvantages outweigh the advantages, can you come up with an alternative view that might be more helpful? If you can, write it down. If you cannot do this at the moment, don't worry. You will find this easier by the end of this section.

## THE PERFECTIONIST PERSPECTIVE OF OTHERS

Earlier in this chapter, we asked you to consider why friends or colleagues might not share your need to achieve such high standards all the time. What answers did you come up with?

Now, for each of the explanations of the perfectionist views you gave in the previous exercise, answer another question: Why does this matter?

For example, if you have put 'My colleagues are contented with a lower standard of work', ask yourself why that matters. Use the 'downward arrow' technique that you learned earlier to get to the root cause of its importance to you.

**Your perfectionist views**

| | |
|---|---|
| *Perfectionist view you hold (1)* | |
| *Advantages of holding this view* | *Disadvantages of holding this view* |
| | |
| **Could you find a more helpful view now?** | |
| *Perfectionist view you hold (2)* | |
| *Advantages of holding this view* | *Disadvantages of holding this view* |
| | |
| **Could you find a more helpful view now?** | |
| *Perfectionist view you hold (3)* | |
| *Advantages of holding this view* | *Disadvantages of holding this view* |
| | |
| **Could you find a more helpful view now?** | |

## Exercise

Now perform a similar test using the next chart, but this time for your colleagues' achievements, where they seem contented with less perfection than you.

Ask yourself the advantages and disadvantages to them of their approach (this isn't about how you see it, but how you

*(Contd)*

think that they might see it). Then, for each person, make a subjective assessment of their self-esteem (where 1 = low and 10 = high).

**Your colleague's perfectionist views**

| View of friend/colleague | |
|---|---|
| Advantage to them of holding this view | Disadvantage to them of holding this view |
| | |
| **Subjective self-esteem rating for friend/colleague** | |
| View of friend/colleague | |
| Advantage to them of holding this view | Disadvantage to them of holding this view |
| | |
| **Subjective self-esteem rating for friend/colleague** | |
| View of friend/colleague | |
| Advantage to them of holding this view | Disadvantage to them of holding this view |
| | |
| **Subjective self-esteem rating for friend/colleague** | |

The big question now is: What does this tell you? Write down (remember the power of the written word against simply considering something verbally) what you have discovered and what it might mean.

## Challenging perfectionist beliefs

Look again at the perfectionist beliefs you listed earlier in this chapter. Now return to Chapter 2, where we covered distorted thinking styles. Can you match your views with any of these styles? Remember that these are thinking errors.

What thinking errors are you making? We suspect that 'all or nothing thinking' might be one of them. Become aware of the others.

Before you can get rid of perfectionist tendencies, it may be helpful for you to understand how you, personally, got them in the first place. While it is quite possible that your parents were always stretching you to achieve more, there can be other reasons as well. Here is a summary of some of the possibilities.

▶ *Parents constantly urging you to do better.*
▶ *A desperate need to please a parent. This might be out of fear, or even love – where, for example, financial sacrifices have been made in order to ensure you received a good education.*
▶ *Sibling rivalry.*
▶ *Scholastic rivalry: perhaps getting into competition with one or two other pupils to 'always be the best'.*
▶ *Feelings of inferiority, either at home or in adult personal relationships that taught you conditional love (unless I am perfect, my family/partner will not care for me).*
▶ *Being abandoned: either 'I'll show them!', or throwing yourself into work or academia as a panacea – something that won't harm or distress you.*

### Insight
Ideas about being perfect come from past experiences that, if we stop and think, are often no longer valid. We therefore don't need to keep following these old rules.

## Exercise

▶ *Write down where you feel your own perfectionist tendencies have come from.*
▶ *Now write a sentence or so describing – based on the reason you have worked out above – why you feel that you need to keep this perfectionism going. In fact, do you?*

Are the reasons still valid, or are you carrying past beliefs along with you that could be more helpfully replaced?

## Exercise

Picking the perfectionist thoughts that you have used in the previous exercises, start making a mental note now of how you might positively and helpfully adjust these in such a way as to keep your self-esteem in good shape.

## Exercise

In the same way that, earlier in this chapter, you weighed up the pros and cons of your perfectionist beliefs – a type of 'cost–benefit' analysis – we would like you to do something similar, using what you have discovered about the origins of your perfectionism.

▶ *Write down what you have decided they are for you.*
▶ *Now do a cost–benefit analysis.*

> ▶ *What are the advantages of continuing to be driven by this?*
> ▶ *What are the disadvantages of continuing to be driven by this?*

Important point: When answering these questions, bear in mind, we are not asking you to list the advantages to you of being successful. We are asking you to consider the advantages of basing your self-esteem on your success.

Is it realistic to continue to think this way? What is the purpose now of continuing to prove something, either to yourself or to others? In other words – don't robotically continue to think, 'I must do things perfectly'. Begin to examine what useful purpose this serves.

Now ask yourself two more things. First, if a friend told you that they felt miserable and inadequate unless they achieved perfection in all that they did, what would you say to them? Second, if you had a friend who seemed to succeed at everything they had a go at, but came across as rather driven and self-absorbed, how would you rate them as someone you really liked?

## Developing healthier values

If you could feel good without always striving for perfection, wouldn't this be much more relaxing?

Develop a healthier value system by really facing where your perfectionism originated from and asking yourself how much you need to keep striving in this way now. Think more in terms of likeability than 'right-ability' as you undertake tasks. Check how you feel as you perform tasks, thinking in this new way. Do you actually feel more relaxed and at ease with yourself?

Perfectionist thinking dictates that satisfaction from doing something is based on how effectively you performed. This actually isn't true, and testing it out will help you make changes to your life that will be very meaningful.

▶ *Start using a chart like the one opposite to subjectively measure this. Use it regularly, as you learn that the greatest pleasure and feelings of satisfaction come from the taking part and not the winning.*

Here is 'one we made earlier', to give you some examples of what you need to do. Construct a similar chart of your own using the blank on page 90 and gradually fill it in.

**Insight**

Let go of the idea that doing tasks perfectly is the only way to feel good.

Letting go of impossible goals and targets is a vital part of increasing self-esteem. How can you ever feel good about yourself if you constantly set such high standards that you will never achieve them and always feel that you have failed?

Measuring your 'feel good' factor

| What you have to do | Rate the satisfaction you hope to get from your performance (1–100%) | How much satisfaction did you actually get? (1–100%) Comment on your rating | Now rate how effectively you consider you performed the task. (1–100%) Comment on your rating | How do you feel now? |
|---|---|---|---|---|
| Mend garden fence | 20% | 90% (can't believe I actually did it!) | 30% (DIY is not my thing, so it's not the best job in the world) | Pretty chuffed! |
| Give monthly presentation at work | 90% | 40% (I do this every month, and so of course I do it well – I expect it) | 90% (I obviously turn in the best performance I can and am good at my work) | Pleased it went well, but nothing more |
| Game of tennis | 60% | 90% (got in a couple of good backhands, and had lots of fun) | 40% (I played poorly, even for my mediocre standard) | Relaxed and happy. It's only a game, I've had great exercise and a drink with my friends afterwards |

Measuring your 'feel good' factor

| What you have to do | Rate the satisfaction you hope to get from your performance (1–100%) | How much satisfaction did you actually get? (1–100%) Comment on your rating | Now rate how effectively you consider you performed the task. (1–100%) Comment on your rating | How do you feel now? |
|---|---|---|---|---|
|  |  |  |  |  |

# 10 THINGS TO REMEMBER

1 *Attempting to achieve everything perfectly is a recipe for setting yourself up to fail.*

2 *In order to understand that perfectionism is simply faulty thinking, understanding where it came from will help you.*

3 *Perfection is not a necessary evil. To improve your self-esteem you need to make changes.*

4 *Remember, perfection is impossible to quantify and therefore all in your mind.*

5 *When attempting to adopt a more balanced view – and not be driven by perfectionist tendencies – spend some time considering others and how they work.*

6 *Consider perfectionist beliefs as thinking errors, rather than rational views.*

7 *Think about the possible outcomes of relaxing your perfectionist views, and give it a go with small tasks or projects, resisting the tendency to 'continue until it is perfect'.*

8 *When you attempt to relax your views, it is a good idea to make a 'pros and cons' list of what you discover.*

9 *Sometimes the drive to achieve perfection can come from a need to be proven right; we feel that our self-esteem will increase if we can show others that our thinking is correct.*

10 *Perfectionist thinking links the satisfaction you get from your achievements to how well you performed them.*

# 4

..................................................................................................

# Defeat low self-esteem by developing self-acceptance

In this chapter you will learn:
- *how to feel okay in spite of yourself!*
- *the important distinction between two types of self-acceptance*
- *how to test your self-acceptance*
- *that it's fine to be fallible*
- *techniques to increase your self-acceptance.*

_____

## Developing self-acceptance

The work you have done so far requires you to look squarely at your negative thoughts and behaviours and to dispute these – to challenge their truth, to look at alternative possibilities, and to check out evidence to support (in most instances) more balanced thinking.

Self-acceptance is a different approach. Instead of arguing with your negative thoughts, you consider them as possibly realistic and truthful – and you may even agree with some them.

Your argument against this way forward might be: 'But that is what I am doing *now*, which is why I feel so badly about myself!'

Actually, that's not strictly true. What is happening now is that when you acknowledge that you may have faults and weaknesses, you do two things (though you may not notice yourself doing this, as it is simply part of your habitual thinking).

1  *The first is that you generalize the specific, for example you decide that – since you don't have a scintillating wit – you are a boring person.*
2  *The second is you decide that having this weakness is totally unacceptable, resulting in feelings of shame and low self-esteem.*

Self-acceptance enables you to conquer your Personal Fault Finder by saying: 'That's fine. I don't mind about these particular things I am no good at. I can accept my shortcomings without diminishing myself.'

If you can learn to do this with calm, inner peace – and even a little humour – the results can be quite spectacular.

**Insight**

Learn not to generalize the specific. Burning the sausages does not mean you are no good at cooking. It just means that, on this occasion, you burned the sausages.

### THE SECRET

The secret is to stop seeing ourselves as a single entity. We are all made up of hundreds of component parts – our skills, abilities, physique, sporting or artistic leanings, levels of competitiveness, intelligence, emotional maturity, personal qualities (such as kindness, compassion, generosity or meanness, good or poor humour) – and many more. To rate ourselves based on each of these individual strengths and weaknesses, we would have very varied ratings for them all. Some might be 8 or 9 out of 10, others perhaps just 1 or 2. If we add up our grand total of individual ratings, the figure we end up with is probably similar to that of most other people – even though our areas of strengths and weaknesses might be totally unalike.

## Exercise

- ▶ *Draw a line down the centre of a piece of paper.*
- ▶ *In the first column write down as many personal skills and characteristics as you can think of.*
- ▶ *In the second column, give yourself a subjective rating out of 10 (where 0 = useless, 10 = my best feature). Don't be falsely modest (you don't have to show this to anyone).*
- ▶ *Just for fun, add your scores up and see what the grand total is.*
- ▶ *What do you think you might discover if you do this?*
- ▶ *This exercise becomes more interesting if you suggest to another friend or family member that they try it as well – using the same basic criteria.*

## Healthy versus unhealthy self-acceptance

*We cannot change anything until we accept it.*
*Condemnation does not liberate, it oppresses.*

Carl Gustav Jung

For many people, the idea that they can accept themselves, warts and all, and not stay plunged in low self-esteem seems a paradox. If you already think you are a loser, then surely accepting this is simply throwing in the towel?

Well, that depends. What is described above is unhealthy self-acceptance. Healthy self-acceptance differs from this in several important ways.

Healthy self-acceptance encourages you to accept *specific* weaknesses about yourself – while at the same time rejecting the idea that having these weaknesses makes you an overall no-hoper. People suffering from depression tend to have an unhealthy lack of self-acceptance, and see themselves as generally worthless. A more optimistic personality will reflect only on specific areas of weakness, and not see these weaknesses as meaning that they are not 'up to scratch' in general terms.

Someone with an unhealthy lack of self-acceptance will consider their weaknesses untenable, and revert to the idea of global uselessness. Healthy self-acceptance embraces acknowledging your weaknesses while not writing yourself off because of them. You understand that it is okay to have skills deficits, make mistakes, get things wrong or not have the strengths of the next person. You say, 'This is called being human, as we all are' and you retain your self-respect.

An unhealthy lack of self-acceptance does not encourage change. It allows its followers to stay as they are, lost in self-criticism and low self-esteem. Their ideas conform to the view that there is no point in trying when failure is a certainty. Or they are 'all talk' – the diet/exercise regime/study course starts tomorrow, and tomorrow never comes. Healthy self-acceptance gives you energy and motivation to change. Accepting weaknesses does not mean *retaining* weaknesses. Change is seen as positive, and accepting your shortcomings without any loss of self-esteem will enable you to meet the challenges it provides you with.

## Insight

It is extremely important to grasp the difference between healthy and unhealthy self-acceptance. Make sure you understand it.

*God grant me the serenity to accept what I cannot change, the courage to change what I can, and the wisdom to know the difference.*

Reinhold Niebuhr

# Exercise

Jot down three or four of your perceived personal weaknesses. Now, for each one, ask yourself two questions:

▶ *'Does having this weakness make me a useless/bad/ insignificant person?'*
▶ *'Am I doing anything towards improving this weakness?'*

Answering 'Yes' to the first question and 'No' to the second means you have unhealthy self-acceptance. Answering 'No' to the first and 'Yes' to the second means the opposite (and well done!)

# Exercise to help you understand self-acceptance: big I, little i

Here is a question for you: Is a zebra a black animal with white stripes, or a white animal with black stripes?

Write your answer down. We'll come back to this in the next step.

▶ *Now look at the big 'I' in the box overleaf. For the purposes of this exercise, this is you! It represents everything about you that makes your totality as a human being. Draw a larger scale version of this big 'I' on a piece of paper.*
▶ *Now think about qualities that you have – ones that you are aware of yourself, or that your family and friends might consider to be your good points (such as intelligent or a snappy dresser). Write a little 'i' inside the big 'I' for each of these.*

▶ *Move on to your weaknesses – again, both those that you perceive yourself to have, and those which family and friends might consider you to have (such as no humour or often arrives late). Write further little 'i's inside the big 'I' for each of these.*

▶ *What about neutral aspects of yourself? For example, you can cut the grass, dress reasonably, are of average height, have brown hair, not turn up late too often, and so on. Write more little 'i's in for these.*

Once you have done all this, your big 'I' should look like this.

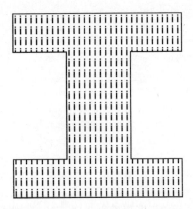

Of all the weaknesses that came to mind, which one currently bothers you the most? Which one makes you dislike yourself the most, feel ashamed of yourself and wish you were different? Now circle one of the little 'i's to represent this.

Now look again at your big 'I' – yourself. The little 'i's within it are the sum total of yourself as a human being: good, bad, neutral – literally warts and all. The circled aspect is just one of many – hundreds, if you took the time to keep working on this.

(Contd)

So does this mean you are a good person or a bad person? A success or a failure? Think about it, and we will look at this further in the next step, when we return to the question of the zebra.

## Insight

Keep in mind that you – along with the rest of us – are a complex person with a limitless number of different facets and dimensions, strengths and weaknesses. You can choose to tell yourself you are hopeless because of your weaknesses if you wish, but that is far from the truth

What did you learn from the big 'I', little 'i' exercise? We hope you will have gathered that you are far too complex an individual to be able to rate yourself in any one way. This is the principle of self-acceptance – you learn not to rate or evaluate yourself, but to appreciate that you are made up of hundreds of different facets that are constantly changing, and defy any sort of generalized, global assessment of yourself based on these.

However, this does not mean that you cannot rate individual aspects of yourself. Indeed, self-acceptance encourages this, as doing so allows you to consider whether you would like to make changes and improvements to these aspects – but without running yourself down for having these weaknesses in the first place. For example, perhaps you would like to improve your time keeping?

### FALLIBILITY

We are *all* fallible. It's what makes us human. We probably make far more mistakes in life than we accept or acknowledge – or even notice. Many of us keep repeating these same mistakes again and again. This doesn't make us bad people or total idiots; it makes us fallible human beings – in other words, *normal*.

*Humans have an incurable error-making tendency.*

Maxie Maultsby

## THE ZEBRA

How did you get on with the question of the zebra? What did you decide? Did it seem impossible to make a definite answer? Thinking about our discussion at present, how might that fit in? Could it mean that it is as difficult to say something is either black or white as it is to say that we are personally useless or perfect, nasty or nice, hopeless or wonderful?

The answer to this is, almost certainly, 'Yes'.

Before we leave the zebra, you will recall that in previous steps we have referred a great deal to challenging assumptions, and finding different ways of thinking about things. The question of the zebra illustrates this beautifully. As you ponder over the question, what about this for an answer?

> *The zebra is neither a black animal with white stripes, nor a white animal with black stripes, but a pink animal with black and white stripes.*

Never stop looking for an alternative way of thinking about things!

## Insight

Fallibility is human. It is fine. It is normal. It simply makes you the same as everyone else.

## Exercise

▶ *Write down two or three weaknesses that you would like to fix, in the light of what we have learned.*
▶ *Rate how badly you feel about having these weaknesses from 1 to 10 (where 1 = very bad, 10 = fine).*

(Contd)

Do you think you have been kinder to yourself with these ratings than you might have been before you read this chapter on self-acceptance?

We hope that, by now, you can consider the idea that you do not have a particular global rating as a human being. Rather, you are (as we all are) simply made up of a huge number of different qualities and characteristics – some of which are strengths, some of which are neutral and some of which are weaknesses. We hope this has helped you see yourself in a more accepting light.

Here are a few more basic illustrations to ensure you are thinking on the right lines.

*Picture a bowl of fruit with all your favourites in it – apples, oranges, pears, grapes, peaches – whichever you like the best. Look at the bowl closely. Wait a moment – there's a bad fruit in there: a grape with mould or an apple with a worm-hole. What will you do? Throw the whole bowl of fruit away, or simply throw away the mouldy grape or wormy apple, and keep the rest? If the latter, then why write yourself off as a person, rather than accepting or working on an individual weakness?*

*Imagine that, when you go into work tomorrow, the receptionist tells you that you are a green frog. What a load of nonsense! Then you go to a meeting, and everyone in the meeting tells you that you are a green frog. How absurd! This is obviously a practical joke that your colleagues are all in on. In the evening you go to the theatre, and at the start of the show the compère asks the audience to look around for a green frog. Everyone turns your way. Would you now believe you were a green frog? Probably not, though you might just glance in the mirror. You would still be more likely to believe that it was a practical joke of some kind.*

How interesting it is that when several hundred people tell you that you are a green frog, you are resolute in not believing it. This is because you are retaining your powers of discrimination. Yet when you make a mistake, you label yourself as totally stupid or useless – in other words, you *lose* your powers of discrimination (which would otherwise be telling you that messing up once does not mean you are a total idiot).

### Insight

Always discriminate between individual weaknesses and your whole being. Don't throw away perfectly good fruit or believe you are a green frog.

Think about what you have read in this chapter, and begin to practise this new, very enlightening outlook. It will help you develop your self-acceptance enormously, as it will give you permission to be fallible and human without seeing yourself as a failure. It also establishes that you are not alone and that we are all quite fallible and may make many mistakes in life. This is normality – not the perfectionism that we can wrongly assume should define us.

# 10 THINGS TO REMEMBER

1   *Self-acceptance is a different concept to self-esteem; it suggests that you can still think very well of yourself in spite of your weaknesses, and that they don't prevent you from being an okay person.*

2   *The advantage of self-acceptance is that it enables you to accept yourself as you are, warts and all, while continuing to improve yourself.*

3   *The way to achieve self-acceptance is to stop seeing yourself as a single entity to whom you give a single 'rating'; we are made up of hundreds of different attributes, with a variety of strengths and weaknesses.*

4   *Unhealthy self-acceptance is rooted in the belief that by accepting your weaknesses you become a weak person, giving rise to low self-esteem.*

5   *Healthy self-acceptance encourages you to look at – and perhaps accept – specific weaknesses about yourself.*

6   *Don't confuse self-acceptance with lack of change. Healthy self-acceptance creates energy and motivation to change; accepting weaknesses does not mean retaining weaknesses.*

7   *Keep the example of the 'big I, little i' in your mind. Remember that you are a complex person with many different aspects to your personality, many strengths – and many weaknesses.*

8   *Never stop looking for different ways of seeing things. Always check for thinking errors – especially making generalizations about yourself that lower your self-esteem.*

9   *It is fine to be fallible. Most human beings are.*

10  *Retain the powers of discrimination and use these in relation to self-criticism; when you give yourself a global 'useless' rating for making one error, you are losing your powers of discrimination.*

# 5

'It's not my fault: life is against me'

In this chapter you will learn:
* *how 'feeling the victim' can maintain low self-esteem*
* *the difference between 'victimhood' and self-pity*
* *that taking responsibility for how you feel is empowering*
* *not to let other people decide how you are going to behave*
* *that 'giving up' is not a good option for self-esteem.*

## The low self-esteem victim

How you perceive what goes on around you, and how you interpret your abilities to deal with issues has a great impact on self-esteem.

### Jenny's story

Jenny was in a troubled relationship, and her partner, James, had recently moved out of their shared home. Although James had treated her quite cruelly at times, having several affairs and behaving in a moody and erratic way, Jenny's self-esteem was so low that she interpreted this as simply a response to her own hopelessness and 'unlovability'.

Jenny spent a great deal of time telephoning and emailing James, begging him to come home. She felt that, without him, she was

*(Contd)*

totally unlovable, and that she needed him desperately to restore her confidence.

In the end, James reluctantly agreed to Jenny's pleading, and returned home. However, the relationship continued to deteriorate, as James did not really want to be there, and continued to see other women.

Jenny's despair came from feeling absolutely stuck. She felt she had tried as hard as she could in the relationship, and that it was James' cruel treatment that made her feel so poorly about herself.

If only James would change, she would feel okay about herself again. Without his input, Jenny felt unable to deal with her life.

This is victim mode: 'I feel so badly due to someone else's behaviour, and need them to change in order to feel better.'

Of course, we may receive an increase in our personal 'feel-good factor' when people treat us well, but we cannot rely on this. The moment we say, 'If he had not done that, I would not have felt this way', 'I only acted that way because of the way she behaved' or 'If she would only treat me with more respect, I'd feel so much better', we are trapped in a way of thinking that prevents us from taking responsibility and making changes.

You will continue to suffer from low self-esteem if you blame anyone else for making you feel the way that you do. You may be right; so-and-so may be rude, may have run you down terribly, may have landed you in it, made you look a fool, or whatever. But it is not about what other people do, it is about how you respond to what they do that decides whether you feel a helpless victim or not.

## Insight

Don't blame others for the way you feel about yourself, or look to others for your feel-good factor. Victim mode will leave you helpless to change.

## Exercise

Think about the last time someone had let you down, for example cancelling an engagement at the last minute.

- ▶ *Did you feel a victim? In other words, did you feel that the actions of the other person were to blame for how you felt?*
- ▶ *Was this a 'one off' or do you often feel this way?*
- ▶ *What might you do differently the next time it happens?*

### Insight
Comments are not always criticism, and criticism isn't always personal.

We briefly referred to over-personalization earlier in the book. Examples of over-personalization are:

- ▶ *A friend makes a comment about liking long hair, and you immediately think they are criticizing your new short cut.*
- ▶ *Your manager tells you that the department is lagging behind completing an important project on time and you assume he is commenting on your own poor performance.*
- ▶ *You suggest to your friend or partner that you get takeaway pizza tonight, and they pull a face and say 'No, I really don't fancy pizza'. What you hear is, 'What a rotten choice – can't you think up anything better than that?'*

When you over-personalize, you erroneously feel that you are personally to blame for the perceived negative reactions of others: 'If someone disagrees with me, then I must be wrong, and that makes me stupid.'

This is not good for self-esteem. You must identify these thoughts and counteract them. This involves using some of the broader thinking skills we discussed in earlier chapters, such as:

▶ *Have respect for the opinions of others, as you hope they will respect yours. You are not stupid if you disagree with them, as they are not if they disagree with you.*

▶ *Distinguish between opinion and fact. However strongly either you, or the person talking to you, believe something, that doesn't make it true. There are many different opinions on almost every subject. Opinions are exactly that – simply points of view.*

▶ *Have confidence in your own views. You don't need to be right all the time – simply having a view shows thoughtful intelligence on your part, and you may have valid reasons/past experiences that mean you are more likely to have formed your opinions in a certain way.*

▶ *Others have their own problems. Your manager may have been under a lot of pressure from his superior to get this work out, and the friend who didn't want pizza may have been preoccupied with a relationship difficulty.*

Remember, other people don't always react in the best possible way. This has nothing to do with you.

### Insight

Start being much more aware of over-personalizing the comments of others, and use your thinking skills to review the situation.

### Exercise

Think back over the recent past to an occasion when you might have erroneously taken something too personally.

▶ *What went through your mind?*

- *How strongly did you believe it? Give yourself a score on a scale from 1 to 10 (where 1 = mildly and 10 = very strongly).*
- *Consider some alternative ways of thinking about this, using some of the skills we have mentioned above.*
- *How do you feel now? Give yourself a score on a scale from 1 to 10 (where 1 = devastated and 10 = fine).*

## Self-pity: blaming yourself rather than others

Every time you run yourself down, you are indulging in self-pity. Not very attractive, is it?

Self-pity is similar to getting locked into victim mode, except on this occasion, you are not blaming others as much as you are blaming yourself – and feeling sorry for yourself. Self-pitying thinking can be:

- *'Why do bad things always happen to me?'*
- *'Why am I such an idiot?'*
- *'I'll never be any good.'*
- *'I always draw the short straw.'*
- *'I can't get anything right.'*
- *'I got a bad deal on good looks.'*

When you think this way, you are allowing your PFF free rein, and not even arguing with it; it is easier to say 'Poor me' and leave it at that.

Don't! Most of us have 'wallowing' periods. Of course, you are allowed these occasionally. But use them sparingly, and be aware that you are choosing to do so. This will give you breathing space to pull yourself together and look at what you are doing.

Self-pity is...

**Destructive**
Self-pity is totally destructive because it robs us of an opportunity
to make changes. It can also lead to depression. What could
be more likely to take you into dark despair than the idea that
everything is against you and that there is nothing you can do
about it?

**Unattractive**
Others may feel sorry for us, but they may also think we are
being self-absorbed and poor company. They may consider
us to be negative pessimists, someone to be avoided.

**Wasted energy**
The energy that we waste feeling sorry for ourselves could be
much better used in problem solving. Self-defeating worry is
physically tiring, without serving any useful purpose.

**Prevents us from moving on**
Self-pity gives us an excuse to indulge our 'stuckness'. We lose
ourselves in self-oriented thoughts instead of action-oriented
thoughts and nothing positive happens. We stay where
we are.

## Insight

Catch self-pitying thoughts as soon as you can. If you need
a little wallowing time, that is fine, but limit it and then
become constructive. Don't waste energy.

## Exercise

▶ When did you last feel sorry for yourself? Why?
▶ Do you still feel that way – if not, why not?
▶ What did you do to stop your self-pitying thoughts?
▶ How did you feel once they had disappeared?

# Taking responsibility for your feelings

One of the easiest ways of getting rid of feelings of victimization or self-pity is to take responsibility for ourselves.

It is not difficult. Look in the mirror and say this: 'I now take full responsibility for my happiness.'

Now say this: 'No one except me is responsible for my happiness.'

There you go! Okay, we do appreciate that it is not quite this easy, but it *almost* is.

## Jim's story

Jim was walking down the corridor at work, when a colleague coming the other way jostled him, resulting in hot coffee being spilled over Jim's new suit. Instead of apologizing, the colleague made a weak joke about it and rushed on, calling back to Jim that he was late for a meeting but that Jim should send him the bill for the dry cleaning. Jim was furious. He was left to clean up the mess, dry himself off, and had to walk into a meeting himself looking a wreck. In response to a jokey comment made by someone in the meeting concerning Jim's appearance, he hit the roof and was asked by the Chairperson to leave the room and calm down. Jim's anger had taken over. He blamed his colleagues for his wretched day and the anger it had produced that seemed to alienate him from several of them.

Was he right? As we are sure you realize, the only person responsible for Jim's anger was Jim himself.

## Insight

No one else can make you feel angry (or any other emotion). You choose to feel that way – and you can decide not to. Engrave on your heart: 'I am responsible for, and decide how, I react. No one else.'

Once we realize that no one else has control over how we feel – and that we have excellent control over how we feel – we can put the lid on negative emotions. You don't have to. If you wish to be angry or upset, be angry or upset. But you are choosing to do so, so make these choices through valid thinking, not using 'I couldn't help it' as an excuse.

With the exception of reflex actions such as a knee jerk or blushing, we can control our responses. It may be hard, but it can be done. This is called 'emotional intelligence', which means that we are able to identify and manage our emotions so that we use them appropriately, rather than let inappropriate emotions take charge of our thinking and actions; this can in turn lead to upset, both for ourselves and others and thus lower our sense of self-worth.

Learn to take emotional responsibility. You will feel much better for it.

## Exercise

Do you always take responsibility for your emotions? Look back over the last two weeks (longer, if need be).

Was there a time when you felt extremely emotional about something? If so, can you recall what thoughts were in your mind?

Did they perhaps include the idea that someone or something had made you feel that way?

How could you look at that now, taking responsibility for it yourself?

## Don't give up

This chapter of the book has looked at our weakness to apportion blame as an explanation for our poor self-esteem, rather than taking responsibility and making changes. One of the main reasons that people don't change – or not as much as they want to – is that they give up. It is natural to hope that when you open a self-help book, a load of fairy dust will fall out over you to make everything okay, or that reading it once will 'do the trick'. But like everything else, it is regular practice that is important.

Giving up can take you back into the victim or self-pitying mode:

- ▶ *'It's too hard'*
- ▶ *'I don't have time'*
- ▶ *'It doesn't make sense'*
- ▶ *'It doesn't work.'*

Dr Robert Anthony (1997) cites research that shows it takes approximately 21 days to break an old, destructive habit or form a new, positive habit. Please keep this in mind.

It will no doubt take you at least that long to gain positive benefits from what you do. While you will understand the book immediately, acting on it is harder. You may read a section and say 'I know that'. But actually, you don't *really* know it.

In order to *really* know it, it must become part of your thinking, your emotions, your actions and reactions. So unless this is the case, reading something and understanding it is not enough.

### Insight

Giving up encourages self-pity. Determine to give your new habits, thinking and behaviours time to develop. Think of 21 days plus – and that is working hard!

In the last year, what have you given up, and why? Write these items down and think about each one in turn for a moment. There will no doubt be good and valid reasons for some, but not for all.

▶ *When have you used any of the negative thought ideas we have suggested above?*
▶ *Do you have any regrets about some of the things you gave up?*
▶ *How has this affected your self-esteem?*
▶ *What do you learn from this?*

To obtain the best benefit, continue reading through this book in its entirety. Then go back to the sections that particularly deal with specific problems you know you have trouble with. Think about these steps deeply, and most importantly, *act* on them.

This is about taking responsibility for your development. This is how you will increase your self-esteem. Don't make excuses; this is what victims do – don't fall back into 'I couldn't help it' syndrome. You can. And you will succeed.

# 10 THINGS TO REMEMBER

1   *Your self-esteem is far less dependent on what is actually going on around you than it is on how you perceive what is happening.*

2   *A victim mentality is one where we have an over-reliance on others to make ourselves feel good.*

3   *Blaming others leaves us powerless to act; by not taking any responsibility for our own feelings, we are left feeling angry and upset at the thoughtlessness of others.*

4   *The biggest trap for the low self-esteem victim is over-personalization.*

5   *Even if you are certain that comments made are both critical and personal, remember that opinions are not facts.*

6   *It is fine to be wrong sometimes! Take more responsibility for how you feel – you will be able to admit to being wrong sometimes without feeling diminished in any way.*

7   *Self-pitying thinking is a variation of victim mode. The difference is that, instead of blaming others, you get locked into a cycle of 'Poor Me'.*

8   *Self-pitying thinking is incredibly destructive; it robs us of an opportunity to make changes, and wastes a great deal of emotional energy.*

9   *While being a victim can seem a constructive way of behaving – gaining sympathy and attention – this behaviour can also be perceived as frustrating and self-absorbed.*

10  *To escape victim mode, take responsibility for how you feel and your self-esteem will increase.*

# 6

Increase your self-esteem through assertiveness

In this chapter you will learn:
- *how you react to situations can cause you to feel good or bad about yourself*
- *four types of behaviour style that you can use to greater, or lesser, effect*
- *how to identify your present behaviour style*
- *how to achieve a good outcome with assertive behaviour*
- *how to use assertiveness skills on yourself, not only with other people.*

## The role of assertiveness in good self-esteem

Does dealing with interpersonal (for example social or work-based) situations that might have a degree of conflict in them cause you to feel inadequate? Do you avoid these situations at all costs, feel you are always on the losing end, or show yourself up in a poor light? Do you currently:

▶ *find yourself getting upset very quickly when others question your opinions and views?*
▶ *avoid discussions that might become confrontational, even though it might mean you don't achieve something you need or want?*
▶ *make a comment you then immediately wish you had not said?*

- *agree with the wishes of others – when really you don't agree at all?*
- *feel your self-esteem constantly dented by your inability to stand up to other people's arguments?*

With good self-esteem these thoughts will disappear. Learning assertiveness skills will give you much increased self-confidence. They will also help you to:

- *improve your image and credibility*
- *behave more tactfully*
- *feel less stressed about confrontation*
- *achieve desired outcomes in a positive way.*

---

## Assertiveness skills

If you do not already possess these assertiveness skills – and most people with poor self-esteem do not – then you will need to practise them a great deal. This in itself may trigger anxiety in some of you, so here is a strategy for making it much easier.

Get a voice recorder with a good microphone, and you can practise ahead of time   again and again if you like – without anyone coming back at you to tell you not to be so foolish.

We often mentally rehearse what we want to say to someone, so how much better to do it so that you can hear how it sounds, and revise it if you need to? Self-criticism in this instance is not another day out for your PFF, it is a positive move on your part. Listen to how you sound:

- *Are you saying too much... or too little?*
- *Are you sounding too weak... or too strident?*

Whatever you don't like, note it, and then have another go again. Eventually, it will become easy and automatic, and even if you still feel nervous, that will not stop you from saying what you want to say, and in the right way.

## Insight
Learning to deal with daunting situations by planning ahead of time, rather than relying on instinct, will develop your self-esteem. You can also practise on your own.

## Exercise

Consider an upcoming situation that you feel nervous about, for example a confrontation with your manager, the builders or a family member.

▶ *Give some thought ahead of time to what you need to say, and then use your voice recorder to practise.*
▶ *Do this several times, until you become more confident.*

## Exercise: Assertiveness questionnaire

Take the test below, which will help you check whether you deal with things assertively or not. Give yourself a score from 1 to 3 for each statement (where 1 = never, or not like me, 2 = sometimes like me, 3 = always, or very like me).

### A

When I have to confront someone about a problem I feel very nervous. ☐
I am easily upset or intimidated by ridicule or sarcasm. ☐
Being liked by people is very important to me no matter what the cost. ☐

I really don't like conflict and will avoid it any way I can. ☐

I find it hard to be direct with people if I think they will not like what I have to say. ☐

*Total score for this section* ☐

## B

I lose my temper easily. ☐

I don't care if people like me as long as I get what I want. ☐

I'll use the tone of my voice or sarcasm to get what I want from other people. ☐

Patience with people is not one of my strong points. ☐

I often wag my finger at other people to make my point. ☐

*Total score for this section* ☐

## C

I remain calm when faced with sarcasm, ridicule or criticism from others. ☐

I am not frightened of addressing problems directly without casting blame. ☐

I am confident about asking for what I want, or explaining how I feel. ☐

I am able to look other people in the eye when dealing with difficult issues. ☐

I feel confident in my ability to handle confrontational work situations. ☐

*Total score for this section* ☐

## D

I often make my point by using sarcasm. ☐

Rather than speaking out directly to make my feelings known, I'll use impatient or 'cutting' remarks. ☐

I show my impatience by my body language. ☐

*(Contd)*

**Insight**

Discovering how assertive you are will help you to spot your
weaknesses and make adjustments to get better results and
increase your confidence.

### ASSESSING YOUR SCORE – WHAT TYPE OF PERSON ARE YOU?

You may have an idea already what your scores tell you. Now let's
put them into a specific context so that you have a clearer idea of
where you 'fit'.

Using your scores from the test, identify which of the behaviour
types most apply to you – the higher you score in a particular
section (A, B, C or D), the more applicable that behaviour type is
to you. You might find that you are a combination of two or three,
rather than always acting in the same way.

## The four behaviour types

The test you took was based on identifying which of four different
behaviour types you adhered most closely to. The types are:

A   *Passive*
B   *Aggressive*

**C** *Assertive*

**D** *Passive aggressive*

---

## Insight

You need to identify your present behaviour type before you can adjust to a more assertive style.

---

Now look at Marian's story, and identify the behaviour styles she was using in the various areas of her life – none of which did anything for her poor self-esteem.

## Marian's story

Marian is 42 years old, married with two teenage children, and works part-time in a local office. Her self-esteem is low, and she feels she is neither a good wife, mother, or work colleague. At work, she feels overloaded and unable to keep up with the volume of work coming through to her. Because she has little confidence in her work skills she says nothing, fearful that her inadequacies will be exposed if she says she cannot manage. The problem is that her colleagues have no idea that she is struggling – they keeping passing more work her way, because she 'never says no'. As a result, Marian doesn't enjoy her job at all, and is constantly fearful that she may lose it.

At home, her teenagers are fairly noisy and self-centred, usually untidy, emptying the fridge as soon as Marian fills it and spending more time with their friends than on their school work. Again, Marian fears her inadequacies as a mother are to blame for this behaviour. In this instance, however, she tries to remedy the situation by shouting at the children, finding fault with their lazy, noisy ways and punishing them with 'no TV' and curfews when they refuse to toe the line. As a result, her relationship with her children is poor. This convinces Marian even more strongly as to what a bad parent she is.

When Marian's husband returns from work, Marian feels annoyed that he cannot see how stressed she is, and does not appreciate the

*(Contd)*

difficulties she has with the children. Instead of saying anything, Marian remains quiet and a little sulky: 'John should be able to tell how I'm feeling' is her view. Unfortunately, John isn't aware, and finds Marian's lack of communication rather hostile. So they spend the evening sitting in different rooms, with no warmth or affection between them at all.

What did you discover? Let's look now in more detail at the different behaviour styles that Marian exhibits, and which you may have found that you possess yourself, as a first step to your teaching yourself to change them where appropriate.

> *To compose our character is our duty.*
>
> Michel de Montaigne (1533–1592)

## PASSIVE BEHAVIOUR

When we behave passively, we tend to 'let things go'. We may totally disagree with what is going on, but don't say anything as we make a negative prediction that things will go against us if we do. If we do speak, we are usually disproportionately deferential, full of premature apology, and back down too easily.

### Insight
Being passive is not being easy-going. It is being a doormat.

## AGGRESSIVE BEHAVIOUR

Bully boy tactics, rudeness, raised voice, shouting, threats – all geared to ensure that the aggressor gets their way on a 'no matter what' basis. You may have behaved this way yourself on occasion, even if you usually exhibit passivity. For the passive person, not saying what they mean – or asking for what they need – can eventually lead to emotional overload. Something 'snaps' and suddenly Sally Shy hits the roof and becomes Betty Bully.

## PASSIVE-AGGRESSIVE BEHAVIOUR

One of the most common examples of this is 'the silent treatment'. You will know just what that is! You may have used it, been on the receiving end of it, or both. Here, we are not being overtly aggressive (so it's hard to pin anything on us) but using silence, sulking, leaving a room when the other person walks in, being deliberately obstructive – you know the routine. Passive-aggressive (P-A) behaviour can also include the 'Poor me' treatment: 'I can see I'll obviously have to write that report myself'; 'I'm the only one who does anything around here'. The objective of P-A is to get one's own way by making the other party or parties feel guilty.

## ASSERTIVE BEHAVIOUR

When you behave assertively, you:

▶ *remain (relatively) calm*
▶ *stand your ground.*

You are also willing to hear the points of view of others, as you don't feel threatened or intimidated by them. Valid counter arguments might make you change your point of view, but if not you clearly stay with what you believe in. You treat others with respect (even if they don't treat you that way). You may be willing to compromise, you speak clearly and you are willing to persist with the discussion until a satisfactory outcome is reached.

## Insight

Understanding these four different behaviour styles will make it easier for you to behave assertively, which will in turn increase your self-esteem as you achieve the results you want in an amicable way.

Write down at least one example, over the last week or two, where you consider you have behaved in each of the above behaviour styles. Most of us vary, rarely using one style the whole time.

Recall how you felt after each event, and rate which felt the best, with regard to how you felt about yourself afterwards.

What do you learn from this?

## KEY SKILLS FOR ASSERTIVENESS

When dealing with tricky situations, we can make the mistake of gearing our behaviour to our dominant emotions at the time, rather than to the outcome we wish to achieve. When we behave assertively, we focus on outcomes and results rather than emotions. Look back to the last chapter when we discussed managing our emotions using emotional intelligence. This is exactly what you are required to do here.

Before you can behave assertively, you need to *think* assertively. This is because, as we have just mentioned, you need to be able to consider the outcomes and results you want, ahead of time. These outcomes and results don't simply include getting what you want. They should also include:

- ▶ *how you feel about yourself*
- ▶ *how you feel about the other person*
- ▶ *how he or she feels about you*
- ▶ *whether the outcome you have worked for has improved your relationship for the future or enhanced mutual respect. In other words, whether it has left your self-esteem in good shape.*

Thinking assertively is important since it starts off the train of situation-emotions-behaviour-outcome, and is a point at which you can maintain control and get the situation to work in your favour, rather than against you.

The work on thought challenging that we have done together in earlier steps is exactly what you need here. For example:

**Situation**
*A debate with your partner about a holiday destination for next year. Your partner is insisting on a venue that you have no interest in.*

**Your thinking**
*Rather than simply feeling upset at the unfairness of your partner's lack of consideration for your views, say to yourself (something along the lines of): 'My partner isn't failing to consider me. He/she is just so keen to go to this place that he/she is hoping I might get enthusiastic as well. I'll attempt to understand what they like so much about it, then express my own reservations, and offer some compromises that fit the bill for both of us as nearly as possible.'*

**Your emotions**
*Instead of feeling distressed, you feel okay.*

**Your behaviour**
*Assertive; listening; acknowledging your partner's enthusiastic preference, while focusing on finding a solution to suit you both.*

**Outcome**
*Agreement reached, which might be a compromise on the venue or the decision that each of you chooses alternate years. A good relationship is maintained and your self-esteem is intact.*

................................................................

**Insight**
Thinking assertively is as important as behaving assertively. It allows you to focus on outcomes and results, rather than simply running with your emotions and 'seeing what happens'.

................................................................

## Behaving assertively

Once you have mastered these skills, you will be able to:

▶ *confront difficult issues with others*
▶ *stay in control of your emotions while you do this*
▶ *stand your ground when the going gets tough.*

Use the following three-step process as a format for negotiation where you need to act assertively.

### 1. Acknowledge the other person's point of view
Most people will expect you to 'come at them' with your own arguments and views, so they will be surprised when you first of all reflect an understanding of their problem.

For example, it might be an unrealistic work deadline that your boss has imposed on you. An acknowledgement might be: 'The work we are doing now is for our biggest client, and I appreciate your concern that we get this project in on time for them.'

Acknowledging sets the scene for dialogue, rather than confrontation. You are actually indicating that you are on the same side as your boss, and share his goals.

## 2. State your own position

Now you have to say where you are in all this. If you really cannot meet the deadline, then you must stand your ground on this point. It is often useful to start this step with the words 'however' or 'but', so that you now have: '...I appreciate your concern that we get this project in on time for them. *However* even working solely on this project and nothing else, the time scale is unachievable, if we are to produce good work.'

## 3. Offer a solution

Sometimes an obvious alternative is not readily available. However, remember that this is about results, and actually there has to be a solution – even if it is that the work does not get done on time. So your thinking needs to move from 'I can't possibly achieve this' to 'What can we do?' and state the possibilities.

Using these steps achieves these vital things:

▶ *It enables mutual understanding of the problems.*
▶ *It gives you the respect of the other person.*
▶ *It prevents you from being forced to accept an unrealistic/ unacceptable/unwanted situation.*
▶ *It encourages a solution to be found that will suit both parties.*
▶ *Your emotions don't get the better of you and cause you to feel upset/angry/disappointed, thus denting your self-esteem.*
▶ *The feel-good factor at the outcome is huge, and excellent for confidence-building.*

## Insight
Think of behaving assertively as a three-step process and do your best to follow this outline.

Now find a situation and practise the three-step process.

You don't need to wait for a major confrontation, even negotiating over a cup of coffee is a good start and will get you used to it.

You may also wish to practise this with your voice recorder.

Think of possible responses you might get, and work on how to deal with them assertively.

## Being assertive with yourself

Learning to be assertive with yourself is as important as learning to be assertive with others.

### Insight

One of the greatest self-esteem boosters around is the realization that most of the things you do and think are pretty well the same as what others do and think.

Look at the example below, and see how the thought processes line up exactly with those you need to use when being assertive with someone else.

> I saved quite a lot of written work on a disk. The next day, I decided to resave, using a different file name. Yesterday's disk wasn't labelled (too lazy!) so now I have two unlabelled disks. I slip yesterday's disk back into the box (basically, to get rid of it) at the same time thinking: 'You lazy so-and-so.

*You are making a real mess of your disks. Most people would be prepared to put the time in to clean up their disks and be much more organized.'*

Using the model from the previous step, being assertive with oneself might go like this:

**Acknowledgement:** *'I appreciate that by putting a used disk back in the box I am creating a possible muddle for the future.'*
**My position:** *'However, I really cannot be bothered about that right now, and it's hardly a heinous error.'*
**Solution:** *'If I need that disk again in the future, I can just wipe the text off then. I've got so many disks I may not use it anyway.'*
**Net result:** *Responsibility taken for action. Feeling very relaxed and comfortable having reminded self that many, many people do this sort of thing – I'm quite okay!*

This is assertive thinking when it applies to you. You have the right to behave however you wish, as long as you take responsibility for it. Most of us sometimes find our fridges full of food beyond its 'sell by' date (some of us still eat it!), have messy drawers we never sort out, tell white lies when turning down boring invitations, fail to tidy up the kitchen for days on end until we no longer have a single clean plate, don't ring our mothers enough, keep the money we found on the pavement, and so on.

We're fine. We're normal. We are behaving just like everybody else.

## Exercise

▶ *Write down three personal issues that consistently lower your self-esteem. For example: 'I get very nervous speaking in a group'; 'My house is always untidy'; 'I'm overweight'. Any three examples will do.*

*(Contd)*

> ▶ *Now ask at least three (more if you can, for a bigger sample) friends, family members or work colleagues whether they ever suffer from these problems.*
>
> What do you conclude from your survey?

## Your assertive rights

> *We are not the only ones to find ourselves at an apparent impasse. As thousands before us have mastered the worst of troubles, so can we.*
>
> Dr R. Brach

Thinking assertively means reminding yourself of your basic rights, and then being comfortable with them. Lists of 'rights' can be very long, so here we just wish to remind you of your right to be a normal, fallible human being, and to ensure you appreciate that this makes you just like everybody else and perfectly okay!

You have the right:

- ▶ *to make mistakes – like every other human being*
- ▶ *to be imperfect – again, like every other human being*
- ▶ *to be in charge of your own thoughts, behaviours and emotions (if these are weird and strange from time to time, you are just like everyone else!)*
- ▶ *to tell others what you want and how you feel*
- ▶ *to feel okay about yourself even when you are not on top of things*
- ▶ *to use emotional responses sometimes, even when they are not achieving the right outcome (we all do that more often than we might like to admit)*
- ▶ *to put yourself first sometimes (yes, take the last piece of cake, don't help out if you are too tired, read a book while your partner is cleaning the car)*
- ▶ *to stand up for your rights – or not; it is your choice.*

Just also remember three things:

1   *Rights carry responsibilities. If you chose the right to go to bed late, don't grumble when it is hard to get up in the morning.*
2   *Others have rights as well. Don't let this deter you from saying your piece, but be prepared for the other person to say theirs as well (and that's fine, by the way).*
3   *See issues from the other person's point of view as well as your own.*

## Exercise

You can practise getting comfortable with your rights by doing the following exercise:

| Think of a 'right' | How you view that right with low self-esteem | How to view it with a more assertive viewpoint |
|---|---|---|
| I have the right to say how I feel | What I have to say is probably less important than what others have to say. I will be interrupted, spoken over, ignored. | My views are just as valuable as anyone else's. I will use my assertive skills to overcome interruptions and persist with my point of view, while acknowledging what others have to say. |

Copy the chart above and fill in three more examples of rights you consider important to your self-esteem. Use the thought challenging columns to counter your concerns with some assertive views.

Assertiveness is a key skill for defeating low self-esteem. Having confidence in your ability to stay with an argument; to negotiate with another or others through to a mutually satisfying outcome; to stand firm when you really don't wish to agree to another's demands – these skills are essential if we are to go into such situations with confidence. As with everything, it really is little more than a matter of practice. So do go ahead: practise as much as you can, and your confidence will soar.

# 10 THINGS TO REMEMBER

1 *Low self-esteem can cause you to find yourself on the losing end of many difficult situations; developing assertiveness skills can change this.*

2 *There are four basic behaviour types: passive, assertive, passive-aggressive and aggressive.*

3 *Before you can behave assertively, you need to think assertively. Remember, everything is about outcomes and results.*

4 *Assertiveness should normally focus on an outcome that is acceptable to all.*

5 *Your behavioural style will play a part in assertive confidence; adopt a manner of calm, active listening, rather than speaking, at the start.*

6 *Acknowledging the other person's point of view is an essential start for assertive negotiating.*

7 *Once you have acknowledged someone else's viewpoint, you then need to state your own.*

8 *Offer solutions, rather than problems.*

9 *Practise using assertiveness skills in minor situations first. This will breed self-confidence and you will be able to become assertive in more difficult situations.*

10 *Being assertive doesn't always mean being on the winning end of any negotiation.*

# 7

# Act your way to good self-esteem

In this chapter you will learn:
- *that 'acting confidently' – even when you don't feel it – really works!*
- *how to develop confident body language*
- *how to develop a confident expression*
- *that how you speak is actually more important than how you look*
- *how to get those significant 'first impressions' right.*

## 'Faking' good self-esteem

> **We acquire the strength we have overcome.**
>
> R. W. Emerson

A good way to improve your self-esteem is to pretend to have it. Your PFF will encourage you to look around at others and point out how confident they are – and how lacking in self-esteem you are in comparison. You are not going to teach yourself now how to check the validity of those thoughts – you have hopefully already done a lot of work on that – but rather to learn how to *appear* just as confident as everyone else – many of whom will be 'faking it' successfully, just as you will be.

A plus of pretending is that, after a while, we don't have to pretend any more. It becomes natural. We occasionally hear the comment 'He/she has told that story so many times now that he/she actually believes it.' This is a version of that. Telling yourself you are confident when you are not is an untruth. But the more you tell it – and in this case, *practise* it – the more you will believe it. You will gradually find it easier and easier, and feel less and less self-conscious. So let's start pretending...

## Master confident body language

When we communicate, over 50% of the message we give comes from our body language, or non-verbal communication. You can therefore send out confident, positive messages without having to say a word.

How would you recognize confidence from body language? How would you recognize lack of confidence from body language? Consider a few ideas of your own, and then look at the list below.

| Non-confident body language | Confident body language |
|---|---|
| Crossing your arms | Open and expansive |
| Hugging your body | Good posture |
| Crossing your legs | Leaning towards someone |
| Placing a hand under your chin | Standing asymmetrically |
| Stooped posture | Relaxed stance |
| Standing far from the other person | Leaning towards the other person |

▶ *Imagine a string running through your body, right up out of the top of your head. Imagine someone pulling this string tight. This will cause you to stand straighter and taller, which always gives a confident impression.*

- ▶ *Clasp your hands casually in front of you – don't fold them across your body. You will look more relaxed this way.*
- ▶ *Give a confident first impression by shaking hands firmly with the other person.*
- ▶ *Moderate use of hand gestures can help to convey meaning when you are speaking.*

## Insight

Use body language to create a confident impression – it will make you feel better, even before you have said a word.

## Exercise

Practise confident body language in front of the mirror at home.

Get an idea of how you look using different stances.

You can also use the list of 'no-no's' to see how unconfident you look in these positions.

If you wish to enlist the help of family or friends, you could ask someone to video you acting out a situation with someone else. This would be particularly useful if you have a special function to attend that is unnerving you.

## Cultivate a confident expression

Conveying confidence and warmth through your facial expression will make connecting with others much easier.

### Eye contact

Eye contact is an important ingredient of a confident expression, but can be hard to get right, especially if you feel nervous – while pretending not to be. It is important because it shows that you wish to communicate with the other person and are interested in what they have to say. So look people in the eye not only when you are speaking, but also when they are – this will also help you to gauge their reactions and respond accordingly. Too much eye contact can seem rather aggressive and overpowering: too little can make you seem nervous or embarrassed. A good rule of thumb is to maintain eye contact for about 60%–70% of the time.

### Smile

Smile! Not only does smiling (appropriately, of course) make you appear warm and friendly, research has shown that smiling will help you to feel more self-confident. Picture someone coming towards you with a warm smile on their face. Nothing could convey 'I'm delighted to see you' more strongly. It is easy to do, and makes a huge difference.

### Relax

Adopt a relaxed and friendly expression. This of course can be easier said than done, and has to be linked, up to a point, to your basic personality. If yours is normally not overly expressive, then simply relaxing your facial muscles will have a good effect and will give your face more expression. To assist you, a useful trick is to drop your tongue down in your mouth, so that it touches the base of the inside of your front teeth. Now let the muscles of your mouth curve into a very slight smile. Not only will you look relaxed, hopefully, you will also feel it.

### Insight

Absolutely nothing lights up your face and makes you look more confident than a smile. Make a truly conscious effort with this, and you will see instant rewards.

## Exercise

Practise facial expressions in the mirror.

Say a few words and sentences out loud and be aware of how you look when you say these things.

Have a go at making statements with a smile (where the content would be appropriate) and see what difference that makes to how you look and how you feel as you speak the words. You will find it makes you feel much more confident.

## Develop a confident-sounding voice

This is not about what you say, but the way that you say it. Nervousness is very audible through the tone of your voice – you may stutter, the pitch may go up or you may speak in a garbled way. When we are anxious – about anything – our breathing becomes shallow as our heart rate rises. This, in turn, affects our speaking voice. Practise controlling your voice and relaxing to reduce anxiety and nerves.

**Slow down!**
It is better to say nothing than to say too much that sounds bad. Return to Chapter 6 on assertiveness to review your confidence in being able to present well without having to say too much.

▶ *Take a few deep breaths to slow your breathing down.*
▶ *However nervous you feel, tell yourself that this will pass.*
▶ *Allow yourself time to relax before you say too much.*

### Not too loud!
Something else that happens to our voice when we are nervous is that it gets too loud, or too soft. Simply becoming aware of this when you are speaking will help you adjust your volume button. You can also ask close family. Take heed of what they say, and make the necessary changes. A good tip is to exaggerate your mouth and jaw movements very slightly. This will give your vocal chords and opportunity to get moving more freely.

### Not too fast!
Another weakness of nervousness is that we tend to speak too fast. This is less common than speaking too loudly or too softly, but you need to check whether you do this. You can use self-awareness, or ask someone else.

In our experience, people are not able to assess themselves when they are speaking too fast. Recording your voice will not help with this, as you will be working hard to speak correctly. Asking a variety of others who you know will be honest with you is the best answer.

### Keep the pitch low
A low, clear voice indicates confidence, while a high voice will indicate nervousness. Practise varying the pitch of your voice while speaking into a tape recorder. Listen to authoritative speakers such as newsreaders, and notice when they especially lower their voices.

### Insight
Work hard on your voice until you feel that it has a confident sound to it – even if you are nervous inside, you will appear relaxed.

## Exercise

Developing an awareness of how you speak requires lots of practice. Do so in the following ways:

- ▶ *Think about your tone of voice when you are in a conversation.*
- ▶ *Spend some time with your tape recorder – most people are extremely surprised by how they sound. It is not usually what they expected.*
- ▶ *Enlist family and friends if you can – both to comment on your speech in different circumstances, and to role play conversations with you in situations you find most difficult to come across well in.*

## First impressions

Whatever happens later, first impressions are the most highly significant factor on which others will assess you – and you them. Think what happens when you meet someone new. You immediately look for signs and signals that will categorize them in your mind. To project confidence yourself, work on the following.

### Dressing appropriately
Don't take the view that how you dress doesn't matter. It may matter to other people, and only an extremely naturally confident person (which we assume you are not) would take the view that they really don't care what others think. You do want to make a good first impression, because it will make you feel more confident. So dress appropriately to the situation. If you really don't know what that is, don't guess – ask.

One tip here – do give yourself enough time to ensure you look as good as you want to. Nothing is more discouraging to good self-esteem than ending up in such a rush that you don't have time to change, comb your hair or apply make-up. Look out here for self-sabotage; the old 'I just didn't have time' is an excuse often used to explain poor appearance, when the thought process is really more to do with 'What's the point, I'll still look dreadful?' or similar negative thinking. In this case, work on *your thinking* rather than *your excuses*.

## Signalling confidence

Ensure that your body language shows the same confidence as your facial expression. During the 'first impressions' stage, you will be judged much more on body language than on what you say, for example: saying 'How nice to be here', while your body language is defensive and your face taut with nerves is not going to wash. People will judge your behaviour more than your words at this point.

Other points to focus on to get the first impression right are:

▶ *a firm handshake; where appropriate (it isn't always, of course) this indicates excellent self-confidence*
▶ *a broad smile; nothing says 'Pleased to meet you' better than this*
▶ *good eye contact.*

## Exercise

Think about social/work situations that make you especially nervous. Now consider the last time you were in one of these situations:

Did you make any conscious, proactive attempt at making a good first impression, or did you simply worry about what impression you might be making?

Now replay this situation. What could you have done – or could you do in the future – to ensure that you make a good first impression, whatever you are feeling inside?

Faking confidence may sound both difficult and insincere. Neither is the case. As with assertiveness, it is all about practice.

Have a go at 'acting confident' in easy, non-threatening situations at first – even just in the local shop, or with the post person or your next door neighbour. Say a little more than you usually would; focus on your voice and especially on your body language. You will soon find that you are no longer acting, and that this is an easy way of being. Thus, what was initially artificial becomes genuine.

This will give you the confidence to 'act the part' in more difficult situations – perhaps at a party or at work – and literally test out what happens. How do others react to you? How do you feel afterwards? Very soon you will have a new 'default' and your self-esteem will rise with this.

# 10 THINGS TO REMEMBER

1 *Think of pretending as practising: after a while this behaviour becomes natural to you and you won't have to think about it any more.*

2 *Never under-estimate the importance of body language; over 50% of your interaction with others comes from non-verbal communication.*

3 *Eye contact is the most important aspect of confident body language.*

4 *A warm smile will not only show confidence, but it will give you confidence.*

5 *Conveying a relaxed and friendly demeanour when you don't feel this way can be hard; practising on your own at home will help.*

6 *How you speak is as important – if not more important – as how you look.*

7 *You are what you wear; your first impression is important, so dress appropriately to the occasion.*

8 *Make sure that your body language portrays the same confidence as your facial expression.*

9 *Visualize past situations when you have felt nervous and uncomfortable and use them to practise and improve your skills of communication and confidence.*

10 *Move from visualization to real situations; the more you fake confidence, the more it will become a simple, easy way of being, so that artificiality becomes genuineness.*

# 8

Body image

In this chapter you will learn:
- *that your body image has little to do with what you actually look like*
- *how poor body image affects you, and where it may come from*
- *how to challenge the validity of poor body image*
- *that shifting your focus away from the negative and onto the positive has a powerful effect*
- *to consider realistic change.*

## Is your body image a problem?

Having difficulty liking your looks makes it harder to accept yourself, but you do not need to live this way. You can change your relationship with your body from one of active dislike to one of being relaxed and confident with your looks.

### Exercise

To check whether body image is a problem for you, answer the following questions. For each question, rate your belief in the statement on a scale of 0–10 (where 0 = not at all and 10 = a lot).

1  Are you uncomfortable with your body in general?
2  Are there aspects of your physical appearance that you really dislike?
3  Do you spend a great deal of time worrying about what you look like?
4  Do you think that what you look like plays a great part in whether others like you or not?
5  Do you think that what you look like plays a part in how much you like yourself?
6  When you think of your looks, do the same negative thoughts keep cropping up?
7  Do these negative thoughts prevent you from enjoying day-to-day life?
8  Do you avoid certain activities or situations (visiting the gym, for example, or going swimming with others) because you feel self-conscious about how you look?
9  Are you considering (or have you had) cosmetic surgery for any part of your body?
10  Do you depend on clothes and/or cosmetics to try and disguise what you consider weaknesses in your appearance?
11  Are you endlessly searching for a new diet, the latest body-shaping exercise, a more flattering hairstyle or dress style?
12  Do you spend a lot of time, effort and money attempting to bolster up your imperfect looks?

Now tot up your score and see how you view your body.

*0–30*
Your body image is good. You don't need to read this section of the book.

*30–60*
Your body image is moderately good, and you are not overly obsessive about it.

*(Contd)*

You have a poor body image and spend far too much time and effort in worrying about it and trying to change your physical appearance.

*90–120*
Your poor body image is spoiling your life. You may wish to consider professional help, if making changes alone seems too hard.

How did you score? Unless you discovered that your body image is excellent, now write down aspects of your physical appearance that really bother you. Do you feel that if you looked better, it would change how you feel about yourself in general? Jot down any ideas you have as to how you might deal with this problem.

## Insight

Your body image has nothing to do with how you look, and everything to do with low self-esteem. This is good news, as low self-esteem is easier to change than how you look.

## How does poor body image affect you?

Many people with low self-esteem also suffer from poor body image. In what ways do you personally feel that your view of your physical appearance affects your life? For example, do you consider it responsible for your not having a partner, or for your relationship being unhappy? Before reading further, note the ways in which your perceived physical imperfections affect you.

You may have come up with some of the following:

▶ *My self-esteem is lowered generally.*
▶ *It causes much social anxiety, as I feel that others are negatively judging my looks all the time.*
▶ *It spoils my sex life, as I hate my partner seeing my body and feel inhibited when love-making.*
▶ *I feel depressed about my looks most of the time.*
▶ *It has caused me to suffer from eating disorders.*
▶ *I never feel really feminine/masculine, so feel less attractive to the opposite sex.*

Where have these thoughts come from? There is no brief answer, rather multiple possibilities:

▶ *Perhaps you were brought up by image-critical parents.*
▶ *Perhaps you had unusually good-looking siblings who received more praise than you regarding their looks.*
▶ *Perhaps you have had a bad experience in an intimate relationship, where a partner you loved and esteemed chose to see fault with your looks.*
▶ *Perhaps peer pressure in adolescence/early adulthood to look a 'certain way', or follow trends in fashion magazines caused you to feel unattractive if you did not meet those standards.*
▶ *Perhaps you developed friendships with people you perceived to be better looking than you and who received more attention.*
▶ *Perhaps you have a naturally negative way of looking at things which allows you to make interpretations, such as 'I would be better liked if I was better looking', or 'My looks are holding me back in life' and so on.*

If you have discovered that you have an extremely poor body image, don't worry. This information will help you to make changes. Let's now make an active goal plan for improving your body image self-esteem.

## Say 'Goodbye' to poor body image

Poor body image is based on negative beliefs and assumptions (remember them from the early part of this book?) rather than reality. For example:

▶ *a negative belief (a fairly absolute view) in relation to body image could be 'Good-looking people are more successful in life.'*

▶ *a negative assumption (more of an 'If... then' statement) might be 'If I were better looking, then my life would be much happier.'*

You can challenge these ideas by finding alternative ways of viewing them; or if your more balanced viewpoint still isn't enough to sway your negative beliefs, you can focus on evidence that simply doesn't support your negative views.

Our goal is to get you to rethink in a positive way both the assumptions you make about your body image, and the importance you attach to it. Once you achieve this, your self-esteem will be in good shape again.

Let's take the belief we gave as an example: 'Good-looking people are more successful in life.'

# Exercise

Develop some challenges to the assumption. How many alternative views can you find? How much evidence can you come up with to disprove this? Write your answers down, and then check with our own suggestions below.

▶ Good looks are very subjective. If good looks are the answer to every good thing in life, why do so many good-looking celebrities suffer from depression, broken relationships and so on?
▶ Good looks are a temporary asset. People who have relied on them when young find getting older a most difficult transition.
▶ We actually get used to people's looks over a period of time. We no longer see whether they are good looking or not.
▶ As many tears are found running down pretty faces as down plain ones.
▶ For many people, looks don't matter at all and that is not the basis on which they judge others.
▶ Being good looking often prevents people from bothering to develop other qualities necessary for a happy life.

Name some of the most successful and well-liked people in history or the current public eye. Were they/are they good looking?

How many disputations did you come up with? Now replace the belief we have questioned with a more realistic alternative.

## Insight

Challenge not only the possibly erroneous assumptions you have about your looks, but also how valid they are – even where they are true.

## GET RID OF NEGATIVE ASSUMPTIONS
## ABOUT BODY IMAGE

What did you write for your disputing thought in the preceding exercise? Hopefully, it was along the lines of:

▶ *'Good looks are nice to have, but they don't account for personal happiness'* or
▶ *'If good looks were all-important, only good-looking people would be happy and successful, yet that is not the case at all.'*

Or perhaps you wrote something quite different, but meaningful to you.

Now we would like you to create a chart like the one below (or simply copy this one if you wish). Use this to record your negative beliefs, find evidence that challenge their truths and then, most importantly, replace them with more helpful beliefs about your own looks and the place of looks in society in general.

**Challenging beliefs about your body image**

| |
|---|
| My negative belief about my body image or the importance of good looks in society: |
| Evidence that disputes this belief: |
| Alternative belief that gives me a more positive view of my body image or the place of physical appearance in society: |
| How do I feel about my body image when I consider it this way? |

Please note that we are not looking for you to provide a complete *volte face* here. That would be unrealistic and unbelievable. What we hope you will find is that you are, at the very least, starting to loosen your negative beliefs about yourself, and are replacing them with ideas that are a little more balanced, and which make you feel somewhat better. It is actually important for you to work in this way, as being able to believe a different perception is vital to increasing your self-esteem.

To help you, here are some generic examples of the types of beliefs people with poor body image hold. Some may apply to you and there may be others that you hold that are not listed here. Use the chart to cover all of them:

- ▶ *'People judge my character by my looks.'*
- ▶ *'My life would be much happier if I was better looking.'*
- ▶ *'I will never be happy until I find a way to change my looks.'*
- ▶ *'I am physically unattractive and I know other people see me that way as well.'*
- ▶ *'My ... (part of body) is ... (too big, too small, etc.) and this is to blame for my low self-esteem.'*
- ▶ *'There is nothing physically attractive about me at all.'*

You will probably have many negative views specific to yourself. Work through them all.

## Insight

Try and approach your poor image from a bigger perspective. If you are agonizing over an aspect of your looks, ask yourself this question: 'What would a starving, homeless person in the Third World say to me if I told him or her that these worries dominated my thinking and prevented me from leading a happy life?' Think about your answer. We are not trying to invalidate your anxieties – which are real and meaningful to you – but simply asking you to place them within the context of what other anxieties there are 'out there' and to help you gain a different perspective.

## Exercise

Fill in at least three different negative belief charts and make sure that you photocopy a dozen or so, to use over the next week or so.

## FOCUSING ON THE POSITIVE

Stories such as *The Beauty and the Beast* or *Cyrano de Bergerac* place a moral behind the story that is not hard to appreciate. If you also focus less on how you look, and more on developing other positive qualities – or appreciating those you already have – others will see the beauty in you.

### THE ERROR OF FOCUSING ON THE NEGATIVE

In reality, those of us who worry about our looks are rarely true 'beasts' – completely ugly specimens without a saving grace. The problem is, we focus on our perceived weaknesses and worry about them to such an extent that we fail to see any of our positive attributes. One exercise that will correct this distorted focus and encourage you to look at yourself in a more positive light is to refocus on your good points.

## Insight

Focusing on the positive may sound obvious, but is *not* always something we do naturally, and we need to work quite hard to retrain our minds to work this way more automatically.

# Exercise

Once a day for a week, write down in your notebook three physical features that you like about yourself. Now, that's a lot of features! We therefore want you to notice your smallest features, for example:

▶ *Look at the shape of your ears ot the size of your wrists*
▶ *Do you have slim ankles?*
▶ *Are your toes well formed?*
▶ *What about your knees?*
▶ *How do you feel about the shape of your nose?*
▶ *You can even make perceived negatives into positives. If you are female and worry about a small bust, think how nice it will be when you are old not to suffer from saggy breasts!*

This is the detail that we are looking for and you must complete three positive features every day for a week.

Once you have done this, repeat this exercise on a weekly basis: one evening a week, write down three attractive features about your physical appearance. You can repeat features, it does not matter. It is the principle of your thinking that will be changing.

Don't make the mistake of thinking that this is too simplistic to be meaningful. It can be a very powerful exercise indeed, with results that are long-lasting. Be pleased that something so simple can have such a strong effect!

## Making changes

We do not wish to ignore the fact that one of the reasons why you may have a poor body image is that the reality you see in the mirror is confirming this for you.

If you strongly dislike how you look, it may be that, as well as an attitude adjustment, you do need to consider an appearance adjustment.

So why don't you? We all know an obese person whose 'diet starts tomorrow' and who never visits a gym. The problem here may be that low self-esteem is affecting their effort rating as well. Or it may be that there are hidden benefits in not shaping up, such as the excuses it provides for general inadequacy or lack of a relationship.

Be honest with yourself. Ask yourself firmly whether any of these situations apply to you. Are you simply failing to acknowledge that there are areas in your life you need to deal with, by using the excuse that your wretched looks are the reason you cannot do so? Ask yourself that question and deal with it if necessary.

If you really do want to make changes, then we suggest that you set achievable goals and work towards them. You can use a chart such as the one opposite to record these.

Using this chart will help you to work out what changes you would like to make, and how you could make them. This is a proactive approach that should result in a 'feel good' factor from both the effort and positive results. Simply making the decision to work on these things should prove motivational and inspirational.

### COSMETIC SURGERY

We would neither recommend nor reject this as a possibility for you. We do recommend, however, that you work through the

## Appearance changes I would like to make

| |
|---|
| Physical characteristic I need to feel better about (e.g. flabby body): |
| What I need to do to improve this particular physical characteristic (e.g. firm up my physique and lose some weight): |
| Now break this down into tiny, achievable steps (e.g. find out about gym costs/locality; make a decision to join; see a trainer about my problems and work out a programme; ask for some dietary advice to accompany the physical work out; set a time limit for achieving my goal; set a start date): |
| Performance record/how am I doing? (e.g. week 1 achievements; week 2 achievements; work within whatever goal plan time frame you have set): |

suggestions we have made before you embark on this course of action. You may well decide that you feel good enough about yourself not to need it after all.

Low self-esteem can lead to 'not bothering' with ourselves; which in turn, can manifest in poor body image. Make an effort to do all you can to improve your physical appearance.

Give this a go. If you feel no better at all, you know at least that your problems lie in other, perhaps unexplored areas and you should return to some of the earlier parts of this book and revisit the skills that will let you dig a little deeper into some of the more basic beliefs you have about yourself and work out what is really going on.

# 10 THINGS TO REMEMBER

1 Poor body image has little to do with how you actually look, but a great deal to do with your low self-esteem.

2 Poor body image is based on negative beliefs and assumptions.

3 You must loosen the strength of these negative beliefs and assumptions by challenging them strongly.

4 When you loosen your old, unhelpful beliefs and assumptions, ensure that those you replace them with are realistic and believable.

5 Consider how much you worry about your perceived physical weaknesses and correct this distorted focus by balancing any perceived defect with an alternative positive.

6 Poor body image can sometimes make you feel like not bothering with yourself; challenge the helpfulness of this view and make a plan to work on your physical weaknesses.

7 By making excuses about your looks you may be failing to acknowledge that there are other areas in your life you need to deal with (for example, social anxiety).

8 Set yourself achievable goals; write down what you wish to change and what you need to do to make this change.

9 Say 'Goodbye' to subjective ideas about looks; it is possible to become so obsessed with physical appearance that you become less attractive as a well-rounded human being, rather than more.

10 Break the vicious circle that poor body image and low self-esteem can create; work on your low self-esteem and improve your physical appearance to the best of your abilities.

# 9

# Becoming an optimist

In this chapter you will learn:
- *how to become an optimist – an excellent way to feel good about yourself*
- *how to develop a more optimistic thinking style*
- *how to avoid thinking in inappropriate generalizations*
- *that depersonalizing events will raise your self-esteem*
- *that becoming an optimist isn't as hard as you think.*

> *Do what you can, with what you have, where you are.*
> Theodore Roosevelt (1858–1919)

Pessimistic thinking reinforces low self-esteem, while optimistic thinking allows us to be more self accepting and retain a 'feel good' factor in the face of adversity.

Yet the only difference between an optimist and a pessimist is their thinking style, nothing else. It is simply to do with how we perceive ourselves and events around us and the interpretations that we give to these perceptions.

For example, if your perception of yourself is that you are dull and uninteresting, your interpretation of possible interactions – '...and therefore no one will like me' – is what cements in your 'feel bad' factor.

We call this 'generalizing'; we talked about this earlier in the book when we looked at distorted thinking styles. For example, if you were required to speak to a group of people at work, your generalized view could be: 'I am so dull and uninteresting as a speaker, no one liked the talk I gave.' This view will put a real dampener on how you think you got on.

However, an optimist might say: 'I suspect I came across as rather dull and uninteresting at the group talk yesterday.' The optimist doesn't *deny* that he may not have spoken that well, but his perception is *specific* rather than *general*. The optimist's interpretation of that thought is more likely to be: 'Some people there may have got a poor impression of my speaking skills but many may not have noticed, and those who know me would not have minded.'

As you learned earlier, feeling good about yourself has much more to do with your view of life than with your circumstances (although not entirely, we appreciate).

## Increasing optimism

You already have the basic skills to achieve this. Having learned to recognize and then dispute negative (pessimistic) thoughts in Chapter 2, you can put this skill to excellent use in becoming a more optimistic thinker.

What do you think about the past? Do you consider that it determines your future? Do you feel that your genes and your upbringing determined your characteristics and that you are therefore 'stuck with them'? These types of belief will discourage you from making changes to your life, so take confidence in the fact that change is possible, and that you will manage it. Take it from us that neither genes nor upbringing are as powerful as your mind.

Let's now look at simple changes that you can make to your thinking style that will help to develop your optimism.

Remember, an optimistic outlook is purely down to your explanatory style and nothing else. Please imprint this idea on your mind.

## Exercise

Do you consider that you would feel better if you saw things in a more optimistic light?

▶ *Think of two or three events coming up where the outcome is important but uncertain, for example: a sporting event you are taking part in or an appeal you have made against an unjust parking fine.*
▶ *Being completely honest with yourself, give yourself a rating between 1 and 10 (where 1 = totally pessimistic and 10 = totally optimistic) for the thoughts you have about the outcome.*
▶ *Are the ratings fairly consistent?*

Does this give you a clue as to what type of thinking style you have?

There is no doubt about it – optimism is good for us. It is also a much nicer way to be, and the thoughts in our minds from moment to moment are more pleasant. Most importantly, it increases our self-esteem. When we start to think that things might turn out well, or that they aren't that bad, we are taking the edge off our negative, self-critical thinking.

Take it seriously – it matters a great deal if your explanatory style is pessimistic:

▶ *You are far more likely to suffer from depression and low self-esteem.*

- *You are more likely to give up easily in the face of setbacks.*
- *You are less likely to achieve success in the workplace because of lack of belief.*
- *It can affect your physical health as you will suffer from stress more easily – and life is simply less fun.*

---

## Positive thinking

So how do optimists view events? What is so different in their thinking? American psychologist Professor Martin Seligman (1998), the leading proponent of the emerging field of positive psychology, has identified what he calls three 'crucial dimensions' that determine the thinking styles of both pessimists and optimists. These are the three 'P's:

- *permanence*
- *pervasiveness*
- *personalization.*

Let's look at these in more detail.

### THE FIRST 'P': PERMANENCE

If you tend to describe bad situations that happen using words such as 'always' and 'never', then you have a pessimistic thinking style. Alternatively, to think like an optimist, you need to use words like 'sometimes' and 'recently'. This is to say the optimist sees setbacks a temporary, while the pessimist sees them as permanent. To illustrate the point, here are some examples:

| The pessimist (permanent) | The optimist (temporary) |
|---|---|
| 'I'll never learn to play the piano.' | 'My piano lesson didn't go too well today.' |
| 'Diets never work.' | 'I'm finding it tough sticking to my diet during the Christmas period.' |
| 'I'll never succeed in life.' | 'My present job isn't doing me any favours.' |

The point is this: when something bad happens, many of us may feel distressed, even devastated, in the moment. However, for an optimistic thinker the distress reduces and then goes away, sometimes quite quickly. For the pessimist, it stays with him or her, even after only small setbacks. After a major setback, the pessimist may never recover. The thinking style doesn't allow the pessimist to see setbacks as temporary, from which he or she can recover, as an optimist does.

### Insight

Start thinking like an optimist – when you have a setback, describe it to yourself in temporary, rather than permanent terms.

### Exercise

▶ *Using the examples given above as a model, write down at least three beliefs that you have which are pessimistically permanent, for example: 'I'll never get slim.'*
▶ *Now write a 'temporary' explanation next to it.*

Practise this often to learn to think like an optimist.

The optimistic thinking style for explaining good events is the exact opposite of the pessimistic thinking style for explaining bad events. An optimist will see good events that happen as permanent whereas a pessimist will simply be waiting for them to come to an end. For example:

| *The pessimist (temporary)* | *The optimist (permanent)* |
|---|---|
| 'Good things never last.' | 'There are many good things in my life.' |
| 'The train is sure to be late today – it's been on time for the last two days running.' | 'It's great that the trains run on time so often these days.' |
| 'Life is going too well – something has to go wrong soon.' | 'I love having my life on track at last.' |

## THE SECOND 'P': PERVASIVENESS

### Jane and Tim's story

Jane and Tim both worked for the same company as graphic designers. When the company lost a major client, it was forced to make redundancies. Jane and Tim both lost their jobs. While both of them were devastated and their self-esteem dented, Jane recovered far more quickly than Tim, and soon found alternative work. Tim, on the other hand, lost interest in everything, and put very little effort into applying for new jobs.

These outcomes were due entirely to Jane and Tim's thinking styles.

When they were made redundant, Jane's view was that her redundancy was a specific event that reflected the company's poor performance at the time.

Tim's view was that his redundancy reflected his poor abilities as an employee and that he was obviously no good at anything.

When our thinking becomes pervasive, we move from the specific to the all-embracing. Instead of seeing one error as an isolated incident (as an optimist would) a pessimist sees the error as an indication of total incapability. In other words, he generalizes the specific. Here are a few examples:

| Pessimist (generalizing) | Optimist (specific) |
|---|---|
| 'I'm unattractive.' | 'I'm unattractive to her.' |
| 'I'm a hopeless driver.' | 'I didn't drive well on the motorway.' |
| 'Exercise machines are a waste of money.' | 'This exercise machine doesn't perform as I'd hoped.' |

### Insight

If you generalize the specific in your thinking, you lose self-esteem in a wide range of areas, rather than just the one area in which events failed to turn out well.

Think about some of the criticisms that your PFF has levelled at you.

▶ *Write down at least three.*
▶ *Now see if you can write alongside a more specific explanation, using the examples opposite as a guide.*

Get used to being far more specific with any criticism of yourself or others. Stop using generalist statements. This is far kinder to yourself, fairer to others, more exact and will help to raise your self-esteem.

## THE THIRD 'P': PERSONALIZATION

We have discussed the problems of personalization earlier in this book. Blaming ourselves for failure is a pessimist's viewpoint. An optimist will assess what has happened and apportion any blame in a more realistic way. For example, you do badly in an exam: a pessimist is more likely to blame him or herself for being a poor student and possibly even give up a course as a result; an optimist will look at the bigger picture. How could you – thinking as an optimist – view this failure? Write down a few ideas before you read on. Here are just a few possibilities:

▶ *your tutor didn't explain the issues very well*
▶ *you had very little time to revise*
▶ *the library was poorly stocked with the books you needed*
▶ *many students fail this particular exam*
▶ *you didn't work as hard as you could have done – you'll need to put in more effort in future*
▶ *you find this subject difficult, but you did your best.*

People who totally blame themselves for every failure will have low self-esteem as a consequence of this. Learning not to personalize events but to look at the bigger picture will help you to think more optimistically and raise your self-esteem.

We should mention here that depersonalization is not the same as blaming others. It is taking a very realistic look at what has happened and then considering all possibilities. As you will see from the example above, the person who failed their exam was actually willing to shoulder some of the blame – 'I didn't work as hard as I could have done' – but he/she can also cite other reasons for failure, as well as thinking constructively – 'I'll need to put in more effort the future.'

### Insight

Challenge negative, pessimistic thinking. Look at the bigger picture, broader possibilities, to explain setbacks. Don't simply personalize them and blame yourself.

## Exercise

Recall the last setback you experienced, in which you felt you were partly or wholly to blame.

▶ *What self-critical thoughts did you have?*
▶ *Using the example above, write down at least four alternative or mitigating explanations for what happened. This can of course include your own contribution, but as a part of the whole, not the total.*
▶ *Review how you feel about the incident after you have done this.*

Is your self-esteem a little stronger from taking this broader view?

If you understand the principles of optimistic thinking, and apply the techniques you have learned to help you to challenge negative, pessimistic ideas and assumptions, you will be on your way to becoming an optimist.

You will react to the normal setbacks of life much more positively and bounce back from major disasters quickly and well. You will achieve more generally, and – most importantly – you will feel good about yourself.

Remember, there is no such thing as an optimist with low self-esteem!

# 10 THINGS TO REMEMBER

1   *Pessimistic thinking is simply a thinking style.*

2   *Optimistic thinking is also a thinking style, but one that allows us to perceive the same events as the pessimist in a more balanced way.*

3   *People are not 'born pessimists'; neither genes nor upbringing are as powerful as your mind and its enormous ability to create positive change.*

4   *The three 'P's taken from positive psychology – permanence, pervasiveness and personalization – are crucial dimensions to our thinking styles that determine their optimistic or pessimistic bias.*

5   *The pessimistic thinking style of permanence involves describing bad events with words such as, 'always' and 'never'; an optimistic thinking style allows us to see setbacks as temporary rather than permanent.*

6   *When something good happens, these thinking styles are reversed; an optimist will see good events as possibly permanent, while a pessimist will be waiting for them to come to an end.*

7   *Pervasive thinking involves generalizing the specific; instead of viewing a negative event as an isolated incident, a pessimist sees it as proof that life is unfair.*

8   *Blaming ourselves for failure is a pessimistic style of thinking; a positive approach is to accept our mistake in a realistic and less self-deprecatory way.*

9   *Depersonalization is simply taking a very realistic look at what has happened, and considering all possibilities from all angles.*

10  *It is not the setbacks in life that reduce our self-confidence, but how we react to those setbacks. Use the powers of optimistic thinking to bounce back from upsets.*

# 10

.............................................................................

# Self-esteem and relationships

In this chapter you will learn:
- *why finding or keeping a good relationship may be difficult for you*
- *the confidence-building skills to help improve your relationships*
- *about the positive power of honesty in relationships*
- *to hold your head high when relationships go wrong.*

---

## Why low self-esteem blights relationships

A major area of our lives that can be affected by our low self-esteem is that of relationships. We may feel friendless and/or we may have difficulty in finding or holding on to romantic love.

At the bottom of these difficulties lie our own feelings of inadequacy: 'I am not especially loveable/likable, so why would anyone really care about me?'

In this chapter, we are not attempting to simplify the many complex problems that exist in relationships, but are focusing solely on issues of self-esteem.

## Exercise

Answer the questions below, and tick any that apply to you.

1   *Are you in a relationship that you worry about?*
2   *Would you like to be in a relationship, but feel that you don't have enough to offer?*
3   *Do you accept sub-standard relationships because you feel you are not worth a good one?*
4   *Are you waiting for your partner to 'find you out' and see that you are really not worth loving?*
5   *Do you tend to 'hold back' in relationships so that your partner does not discover all your faults and weakness?*
6   *Do you actively avoid relationships because you cannot conceive of yourself as lovable?*
7   *Do you tend to sabotage perfectly good relationships on the basis that it will all end in tears at some point, so better now than later?*
8   *Do you spoil relationships by being very needy?*
9   *Do you pick arguments simply to rouse your partner to show that he or she 'really cares'?*
10  *Do you feel despondent that you will ever feel really loved and content?*

Unfortunately, if you ticked even one of these statements, your self-esteem is sabotaging your relationship chances. Confidence in relationships comes only from confidence in ourselves. We need to learn to like ourselves first.

A common problem is that, where our self-esteem is low, we look for someone else to make us feel better. We decide that if we are liked and loved by others, then we will like and love ourselves.

This thinking error is what leads to relationship failure. For if we don't like ourselves, why would we expect others to like us?

In the previous section we discussed being a good listener. The secret of finding and retaining a good relationship is very similar. We need to stop thinking and worrying about ourselves, and develop more of a focus on others.

## Insight

We need to love ourselves if we want others to love us as well. In relationship terms, this means offering something, rather than simply hoping to take something from a friendship or romance.

## Exercise

What do you believe prevents you from finding or retaining a happy relationship? Write your answers down. Do the answers relate more to faults you feel *you* have that make you unlovable, or do they relate more to faults in most people you meet that make *them* unlovable?

## How to gain confidence in your relationship

Many people say that they have difficulty finding a relationship. This can be because we expect too much of other people – especially if we need them to enhance our self-esteem. They have to be pretty special to be able to do that for us.

To increase your self-esteem, you need to adjust your thinking and practise changing your behaviour. Begin by taking a real interest in the people you meet.

This is an excellent skill for self-esteem. Building on the work in the last section, you are basically 'off-focusing'. Instead of thinking about *yourself*, *your* needs, *your* inadequacies, you focus on who you are with and ensure you find out about them.

This will help you build confidence in your own likeability, and is very good practice for relationship-building.

## GOOD COMMUNICATION

When we communicate well with friends or our partners, we feel confident and good about ourselves. Poor communication can make us angry and upset, or fuels feelings of inadequacy.

In your closest relationships this means – yet again – listening well.

When we are in very intimate relationships – and no longer on our 'best behaviour' – we spend a great deal of time either talking or waiting. We are either saying our piece or waiting for our partner to finish speaking so that we can say our next piece. We don't actively listen.

### UNDERSTANDING

Communicating well with your partner will give you confidence. You will communicate well if you first listen to what they have to say (rather than believing that what you have to say is more important) and then ensuring that you have understood it by commenting in a constructive way.

For example, if James tells Mary that he is unhappy that she doesn't like him spending time in the pub with his friends, she will do better not to respond with a statement, such as: 'You obviously prefer being there rather than here with me.' A better response would be to understand what he is saying and express how she feels, so that he is given the opportunity to find a solution. For example: 'I appreciate that you like to be able to relax after work with your friends sometimes, but I miss you as well. How can we resolve this?'

Showing interest and communicating well through listening
and understanding will kick-start new relationships, enhance
those you already have and give you lots of confidence.

## Exercise

With everyone you come into contact with today, either at
work, at home or socially, speak less and listen more.

Be aware of the outcomes.

How do you feel about yourself and what is your perception
of how others view you when you do this?

### AN EASY TRICK – JUST BE NICE!

How simple is that?! Let's explain it this way... One of the
difficulties in relationships is our high expectations. The lower our
self-esteem, the higher our expectations are. We 'need' our partner
to do all the right things:

- ▶ *to notice if we're unhappy*
- ▶ *to buy the right birthday present*
- ▶ *to spot our new haircut or the weight we have lost*
- ▶ *in other words, we need them to make us feel good about
  ourselves.*

The result of these demands can be disappointment, and
disappointment will confirm our worst fears; we have either made a
bad choice of partner or we are not worth treating lovingly and well.

Where is the focus here? Yes, we're back chasing our self-esteem
again. Looking to achieve good self-esteem from our partner in

our relationship, failing to find it, becoming distressed, feeling worse. We have again become totally self-focused. It's all about US again.

> *The secret of a good relationship is not finding the right person, but being the right person.*

Anon

Test this out: for two days – as a start – stop being needy. This means that you stop seeing life in your terms, and think only about what you can do for your partner. This is not being a wimp, this is a genuine exercise in discovering whether you can actually feel better about yourself by behaving nicely rather than in a needy way.

At the end of the two days, ask yourself the following questions:

- ▶ *How do I feel about myself and my behaviour (irrespective of the responses I received)?*
- ▶ *Do I feel better about myself – have I given it my best, even in adverse circumstances?*
- ▶ *Have I noticed any change in my partner? Has he or she appreciated my behaviour, or taken it for granted?*
- ▶ *Would I feel better if I continue to make these efforts?*
- ▶ *How might this affect my self-esteem?*

You may say that you have a tricky partner – who does not deserve warmth and kindness – and will take you for granted if you do. Unfortunately, it is not in the remit of this book to deal with difficult relationships, and you may have to make your own decisions here. We are attempting to help you find ways to increase your own self-esteem within your relationship – *even if this eventually encourages you to have the confidence to leave a relationship that is unrewarding.*

Review the situation two days afterwards. Resolve to do a further two days if you can – and then more and more, as you cement your confidence and get back what you give.

## Using openness and honesty

When our self-esteem is low, it is easy to sabotage relationships with defeatist behaviour. This can include assuming the worst, focusing on the negative, not allowing yourself to feel exposed in case you get hurt – the type of behaviour that means your partner never really gets to know the real person behind all this smoke screen.

To succeed in dislodging low self-esteem associated with any area of your life, you need to take a risk. You can:

▶ *stretch yourself a little*
▶ *change defeatist behaviours*
▶ *do something new without being certain of the outcome.*

It is no different with intimate relationships. A saying worth remembering is: 'To risk nothing, is to risk everything.' Yes, you might get hurt if a relationship goes wrong but you can learn to cope, and can save your energies to deal with that if it happens. Don't waste your energies on it now. You can risk:

▶ *being open*
▶ *speaking from your heart*
▶ *letting your partner know the real you.*

Think about the following. With whom do you feel most at ease?

a *Someone who tells you only 'the good stuff' about themselves and their life, or*
b *A person who is open about their faults and weaknesses?*

If you chose **b** – why?

▶ *Do you feel more comfortable with someone who is self-effacing – willing to laugh at themselves and confess their mistakes, or do you prefer someone who never makes mistakes?*

▶ *Do you appreciate someone who is willing to confide intimate details about their life, or do you prefer not to know?*

▶ *Do you actually feel flattered that someone sees you as someone they can tell these things to?*

Based on the above, if you reverse the positions, and become the open, honest, intimate detail risk-taker, is your partner likely to feel more loving and at ease with you, or less?

## Insight

Take the risk of being open and honest in your relationships. Your self-esteem will increase, not decrease and your relationship will develop positively.

Remember, to risk nothing is to risk everything. Take a risk with openness and honesty. The boost it will give your confidence to discover how much more you are loved – rather than how much less you are loved – will be well worth it.

## Exercise

Each day this week, tell someone close to you – your partner if you have one, your best friend or a work colleague – one aspect about yourself that they did not know before. Be aware of how easy or difficult you found that, and any notable response from the person you told. Build being more open into your daily life, until you feel quite comfortable and confident doing so.

# Surviving a break-up with your self-esteem intact

*We are never so helplessly unhappy as when we lose love.*

Sigmund Freud

When a relationship ends – and not of our choosing – it can have the most devastating effect on our self-esteem, if we allow it. The pain of losing someone we love can be heartbreaking and any extra pain caused by thinking we are worthless and unlovable can be extremely hard to bear. It's no wonder we may feel depressed.

In some cases, people never put themselves through these negative ideas and emotions again. They see the ending as a sign that they are not worthy of being loved and that this is how things would undoubtedly end on another occasion.

While accepting heartbreak, you don't have to allow your self-worth to be called into question.

## USE YOUR THINKING SKILLS

One of the most important skills is not to generalize the specific. This particular relationship did not work out. This particular person turned out not to be right for you. This does not mean you are unlovable. Use your evidence-finding skills and ask yourself these questions:

- ▶ *Have you ever been loved before?*
- ▶ *Who else has loved you in your life?*
- ▶ *What does this mean about your lovability?*

## Insight
If you can keep your dignity no matter how your heart is breaking, you will be able to maintain your self-esteem.

Remember, you have choices in these situations. You could do the following:

► *Don't say too much. It's easy to pour out invective, go into detail about misunderstandings, how you feel, what happened when and so on. Don't do this. It is too much information, it will not be heard and it will not make any difference. Say as little as possible and you will be respected for this, plus – and most importantly – you will respect yourself.*

► *If you still love the person, tell them so, but with grace and dignity and without asking anything in return.*

► *Determine not to contact them, not to beg or plead or behave in any way that you may regret later and will cause you more pain and regret. There is more chance that your lost love will contact you at some point if they hear nothing from you (if that is what you want, of course).*

► *Be certain that, however your heart is breaking, you have done nothing wrong and should hold your head up high. The difference this type of dignity will make to your self-esteem in the aftermath will be quite spectacular.*

You cannot always keep the person you loved, but you can keep your self-esteem if you act with dignity.

## Exercise

If you have found yourself in this situation in the past, look back at how you dealt with it.

What lowered your self-esteem the most?

If it was to do with your own behaviour, what could you learn from that?

Intimate relationships can invoke the highest of emotions. In turn, high emotion can overturn rational behaviour; we can find ourselves failing to manage our emotions at all, but rather letting them manage us and often living to regret it – and living with the lower self-esteem that can stem from this. If you are in a relationship where you lack confidence – or find that this is a 'usual pattern' for you – do please reread this chapter, and ensure that you both understand and then put into practice what you have learned. The difference in your self-esteem – and consequently the quality of your relationships – will surprise you.

# 10 THINGS TO REMEMBER

1  *Low self-esteem blights relationships; if you don't like yourself very much, why should anyone else?*

2  *Recognize that perhaps you feel safer on your own because you will not be judged and found wanting and start working on improving your self-esteem as a better way forward.*

3  *Stop thinking and worrying about yourself and develop more of an interest in others.*

4  *It is vital that you offer something – rather than simply hoping to take something – from a friendship or romance.*

5  *Take a real interest in the people you meet; you don't need to be a good conversationalist, just a good and genuinely interested listener.*

6  *Curb your neediness; this requires too much of a partner.*

7  *Low self-esteem can prevent you from exposing your 'true self' to your partner; you need to take risks and open up.*

8  *Openness and honesty are valued traits; embrace them.*

9  *Don't allow your self-worth to be called into question by the end of a relationship; you are not unlovable – things were just not right on this occasion.*

10  *Your self-esteem will remain high if you act with dignity and elegance when a relationship ends.*

# 11

....................................................

# Developing emotional strength

In this chapter you will learn:
- *how developing emotional strength will increase your self-esteem*
- *the characteristics of emotional strength*
- *how to measure emotional strength within yourself*
- *how you can improve your own resilience*
- *how to step out of your comfort zone and increase your confidence.*

Being emotionally strong implies having (or developing) the ability to stand firm in the face of adversity and to respond strongly to emotions that might be upsetting or difficult to deal with. Another way of expressing emotional strength is to describe yourself as resilient.

Your self-esteem will increase enormously as you learn not to crumble internally or negatively personalize difficult events, but rather to stand firm and – with confidence – put things right.

## What is resilience?

When something goes wrong, do you bounce back or do you fall apart? Those with resilience harness their inner strength and tend to rebound more quickly from a setback or challenge – whether it's a job loss, an illness or the death of a loved one.

In contrast, people who are less resilient may dwell on problems, feel victimized, become overwhelmed and turn to unhealthy coping mechanisms – such as substance abuse. They may even be more inclined to develop mental health problems. Resilience won't necessarily make your problems go away. But it can give you the ability to see past them, have the confidence to find enjoyment in life and handle future stressors better.

If you aren't as resilient as you'd like, teach yourself to become more so and your self-esteem will rise alongside this.

There is a great deal of research being carried out worldwide into resilience, what it means and how it can be fostered and developed. Civil war, famine and lack of the most basic resources (such as clean water) require people to survive in the face of enormous difficulties. Helping these people to develop resilience will quite literally save lives, which is why government health agencies are willing to spend quite large sums of money researching it and understanding the key strategies for developing it.

## Insight

Although the impetus for resilience research originally came from research into 'at risk' populations, what has ultimately emerged from this research is a picture of the building blocks of emotional good health that is relevant to us all.

### UNDERSTANDING RESILIENCE

Here are some definitions of resilience, as it has been defined by a variety of researchers in the field.

▶ *'Remaining competent despite exposure to misfortune or stressful events.'*
▶ *'A capacity which allows a person... to prevent, minimize or overcome the damaging effects of adversity.'*
▶ *'The capacity some people have to adapt successfully despite exposure to severe stressors.'*

- ▶ *'The human capacity to face, overcome, and even be strengthened by the adversities of life.'*
- ▶ *'The process of, capacity for, or outcome of successful adaptation despite challenging or threatening circumstances.'*

Resilience is the ability to adapt well to stress, adversity, trauma or tragedy. It means that overall, you remain stable and maintain healthy levels of psychological and physical functioning in the face of disruption or chaos.

If you have resilience, you may experience temporary disruptions in your life when faced with challenges. For example, you may have a few weeks when you don't sleep as well as you typically do. But you're able to continue with daily tasks, remain generally optimistic about life and rebound quickly.

Resilience isn't about toughing it out. It doesn't mean you ignore feelings of sadness over a loss – it actually means becoming more aware of them and then being able to deal with them rather than feel overwhelmed and incapable. Nor does it mean that you always have to be strong and that you can't ask others for support – in fact, reaching out to others is a key component of nurturing resilience in yourself.

Resilience doesn't mean that you're emotionally distant, cold or unfeeling, rather the opposite. It increases your self esteem so that you are far more at ease talking openly to others.

Resilience protects you against developing such conditions as depression, anxiety or post-traumatic stress disorder. Actively working to promote your mental well-being is just as important as protecting yourself from such physical conditions as heart disease and diabetes. Resilience may help offset certain risk factors that make it more likely that you'll develop a mental illness, such as lack of social support, being bullied or previous trauma.

People who are more resilient have the ability to say to themselves: 'Okay, this bad thing happened and I can either dwell on it or I can do something about it.'

Resilience can help you endure loss, chronic stress, traumatic events and other challenges. It will enable you to develop a reservoir of internal resources that you can draw on, and it may protect you against developing some mental illnesses. Resilience will help you survive challenges and even thrive in the midst of chaos and hardship.

**Insight**

Resilient individuals are able to cultivate a sense of forgiveness and – regardless of the setback or slight – they're able to box it up, put it in a package and let go of it.

## The characteristics of resilience

American psychologist and researcher Nancy Davis identified six areas of competence that she defined as characteristics of resilience. She identified them as follows.

### Exercise

As you read through these characteristics, think hard about those which may already apply to you or where, having now been identified to you, you could absorb them and develop them yourself.

1  **Physical**
   *Good health*
   *Easy temperament*

2  **Spiritual**
   *Having faith that one's own life matters*
   *Seeing meaning in one's life even in pain and suffering*
   *Sense of connection with humanity*

3 **Moral**
   *Ability and opportunity to contribute to others*
   *Willingness to engage in socially and/or economically useful tasks*

4 **Emotional**
   *Ability to identify and control emotions*
   *Ability to delay gratification (patience)*
   *Realistically high self-esteem*
   *Creativity*
   *Sense of humour*

5 **Social/relational**
   *Ability to form secure attachments*
   *Basic trust*
   *Ability and opportunity to actively seek help from others*
   *Ability to make and keep good friends*
   *Ability to empathize*
   *Possess good other awareness*

6 **Cognitive (thinking skills)**
   *Possess a good ability to manage your emotions*
   *Possess good communication skills*
   *Be open to a variety of ideas and points of view*
   *Have a capacity to plan*
   *Be able to exercise foresight*
   *Possess good problem-solving abilities*
   *Be able to take and use initiative*
   *Possess good self-awareness*
   *Be able to appreciate and assess the consequences of actions taken*

**It is crucial to remember that, given an adequate facilitating environment, people have the capacity for positive change and for the development of at least some characteristics of resilience throughout their lives.**

Nancy Davis (psychologist)

# Exercise: test your resilience

Here is a tool to measure your resilience – your ability to bounce back from stressful situations. People who are resilient recover quickly from disruptive change, illness, or misfortune without being overwhelmed or acting in destructive ways.

The tool uses the values you enter to calculate your score. The calculation is based on personality factors – such as flexibility, self-confidence, creativity, and ability to learn from experience – that make people more resilient.

Look at each statement below and write beside it the number that most closely describes how much you agree with it, from 1 to 5 (where 1 = strongly disagree and 5 = strongly agree).

1   *I adapt quickly.*
2   *I'm good at bouncing back from difficulties.*
3   *I'm able to recover emotionally from losses and setbacks.*
4   *I can express my feelings, let go of anger, overcome discouragement and ask for help.*
5   *I feel self-confident, enjoy healthy self-esteem, and have an attitude of professionalism about my work.*
6   *In a crisis or chaotic situation, I calm myself and focus on taking useful actions.*
7   *I'm optimistic. I see difficulties as temporary, expect to overcome them, and believe things will turn out well.*
8   *I'm good at solving problems logically.*
9   *I can think up creative solutions to challenges.*
10  *I trust my intuition.*
11  *I'm curious, ask many questions, want to know how things work and experiment with solutions.*

12  *I'm playful, find the humour in tough situations and can laugh at myself.*

13  *I consistently learn from my experience and from the experience of others.*

14  *I'm very flexible.*

15  *I feel comfortable with myself.*

16  *I try to anticipate problems to prevent them and I expect the unexpected.*

17  *I'm a good listener, am empathetic and 'read' people well.*

18  *I'm non-judgemental and can adapt to different personality styles.*

19  *I'm able to tolerate uncertainty about situations.*

20  *I'm good at making things work well.*

21  *I'm often asked to lead groups and projects.*

22  *I've been made stronger and better by difficult experiences.*

23  *I keep going through tough times and have an independent spirit.*

24  *I've found benefits in bad experiences.*

Now total your score.

A score between 100–120 suggests that you are extremely resilient.

A score between 75–99 suggests that you normally bounce back quite well from adversity.

A score between 50–75 suggests that your resilience may wobble occasionally.

A score below 50 suggests that you find recovering from difficulties quite hard and need to develop your personal strengths to deal with what life throws at you.

## Develop emotional strength by improving resilience

Here are a range of useful tips and strategies to help you develop emotional strength and improved resilience. Take a pen and paper, and as you read through the list below, make a written note of any of the points that you may need to work on. Keep this by you to use later in the chapter with further exercises.

### Get connected
Build strong, positive relationships with family and friends who can listen to your concerns and offer support. Get involved in groups or volunteer organizations that give you an opportunity to help others. Relationships like these can also fulfil your need for a sense of belonging and help banish loneliness.

### Use humour and laughter
Remaining positive or finding humour in distressing or stressful situations doesn't mean you're in denial. Humour is a helpful coping mechanism. If you simply can't find humour in your situation, turn to other sources for a laugh, such as a funny book or movie.

### Learn from your experiences
Recall how you've coped with hardships in the past, either in healthy or unhealthy ways. Build on what helped you through those rough times and don't repeat actions that didn't help. Work out what lessons you learned and how you'll apply them when faced with similar situations.

### Remain hopeful and optimistic
When you're in the middle of a crisis, it may seem as though things will never get better. While you can't change the events, look toward the

future, even if it's just a glimmer of how things might improve. Find something in each day that signals a change for the better. Expect good results. Believing things happen for a reason may help sustain you.

## Take care of yourself
Tend to your own needs and feelings, both physically and emotionally. This includes participating in activities and hobbies you enjoy, exercising regularly, getting plenty of sleep and eating a well-balanced diet.

## Accept and anticipate change
Be flexible. Change and uncertainty are part of life. Expecting changes to occur makes it easier to adapt to them, tolerate them, and even welcome them.

## Work toward goals
Do something every day that gives you a sense of accomplishment. It doesn't have to be a major goal, such as getting the college degree you've been meaning to pursue. Even small, everyday goals are important, such as finishing a work project or making a difficult phone call. Having goals helps direct you toward the future.

## Take action
Don't just wish your problems would go away or try to ignore them. Chances are they won't disappear on their own. Instead figure out what needs to be done, make a plan to do it, and then take action to resolve your problems.

## Learn new things about yourself
Look back on past experiences and think about how you've changed as a result. You may be stronger than you thought. You may have gained a new appreciation for life. If you feel worse as a result of your experiences, think about what changes might help to improve things. Explore new interests, such as taking a cookery class or joining an interest group.

## Think better of yourself
Congratulate yourself for enduring hard times, loss or stress. Be proud of yourself. Trust yourself to solve problems and make

sound decisions. Think positively about yourself. Nurture your self-confidence and self-esteem so that you increase your belief in being a strong, capable and self-reliant person who can withstand hardships and criticism. This will give you a sense of control over events and situations in your life and confidence in your ability to manage them well.

## Insight

Additional ways of strengthening resilience may be helpful. For example, some people write about their deepest thoughts and feelings related to a trauma or other stressful events in their life. Meditation and spiritual practices help some people build connections and restore hope.

### Maintain perspective

This doesn't mean comparing your situation to that of somebody you think may be worse off than you. Rather, it means looking at your situation in the larger context of your own life and of the world around you. Keep a long-term perspective and know that your situation can improve if you actively work to make it better.

## Sources of resilience

The International Resilience Project defines resilience in terms of three sources: I HAVE (social and interpersonal supports); I AM (inner strengths) and I CAN (interpersonal and problem-solving skills).

## Exercise

Do you have – or do you need to create – these three sources of resilience? Take a look at each of these sources and place a tick against those which you personally consider are already present in your life.

**I have...**

people around me I trust and who love me no matter what

people who set limits for me so I know when to stop before there is danger or trouble

people who show me how to do things right by the way they do things

people who want me to learn to do tasks on my own

people who help me when I am sick, in danger or need to learn.

**I am...**

a person people can like and love

glad to do nice things for others and show my concern

respectful of myself and others

willing to be responsible for what I do

sure things will be alright.

**I can...**

talk to others about situations that frighten or bother me

find ways to solve problems I face

control myself when I feel like doing something not right or dangerous

figure out when it is a good time to talk to someone or to take action

find someone to help me when I need it.

*(Contd)*

For a person to be resilient, he or she needs to have more than one of these strengths. For example, if someone has people whom they can turn to for support (I HAVE), but has low self-esteem (I AM), and does not have the capacity solve problems (I CAN), they will not be resilient.

Look at where you have placed your ticks. Are they spread well across the three sources? This will indicate higher resilience than if they are bunched together under one source.

## Understanding resilience as a process

Resilience is not an attribute of an individual, as this would imply a fixed and unchanging invulnerability that some have and some do not. Rather it is a complex *process* involving both internal cognitive and personality factors and the functioning of external protective factors, such as caring adults. Resilience is also a normal, understandable process. It arises from normal, human adaptational systems, such as the ability to rationally solve problems, the capacity to regulate emotion and the ability to form close, supportive ties with others. It is only when these systems are damaged or overwhelmed by lack of belief and low self-esteem that natural human resilience fails.

## Exercise

This exercise will help you develop personal resilience in specific areas (refer to the list you made earlier in this chapter). To develop resilience, you will need to practise.

- ▶ *Write down four aspects of your life in which you consider yourself to be resilient in general, or have specifically shown resilience recently.*
- ▶ *Now do the same for areas of your life where you consider you would like to develop your resilience.*
- ▶ *Now answer the following question: When you look at the parts of your life where you have shown resilience, what specific attributes have you shown, for example: tenacity, emotional control, ability to see the problem and the solution? Use examples from what you have read so far to give yourself some ideas. Now write them down.*
- ▶ *Look now at the areas of your life where you would like to develop your resilience. Would any of the attributes you have identified already help you? If not, what further attributes would you need to develop? (Again, look for examples in what you have read so far.)*

## Developing resilience

Developing resilience means, most importantly, stepping outside your comfort zone. It means being willing to try a little harder, carry on when you might previously have given up, being willing to feel emotions such as anxiety and fear and yet not back down.

It also means practice. The only reason most people do not master new skills as well as they would like is that they simply have not done them often enough for long enough. Keep practising and the difficult becomes possible, and the possible becomes easy.

It also means positive self-talk! American psychologist Christine Padesky – who has spent some time researching and developing a model for improving resilience – has compiled a list of 'summary statements' which give positive enhancement to resilience competencies, for example:

| Area of competence | Suggested summary statement |
|---|---|
| Problem-solving attitude | These are just problems to solve. |
| Problem-solving strategy | If I break it down into smaller bits I can handle it better. |
| Commitment to persistence | If I just stick to it – if I don't give up – I'll figure something out. |
| Inspirational metaphor | Water dripping on stone over time can actually break through. |
| Attitude of creative tenacity | I'll find another way. |
| Flexibility principle | It helps if I look at it from another perspective. |
| Social support | I can get help from others. |
| Emotional resilience | Even though I feel…, over time I can find a way to cope. |
| Spiritual focus | I will focus just on what is important. |
| Connection with others | I take comfort from knowing other people struggle with this too. |
| Focus on success instead of failure | It helps to see how far I have come or have been able to do so far. |
| See challenges instead of problems | I've got to be more creative and flexible. |
| Focus on possibilities not difficulties | Rome wasn't built in a day. |
| Use of humour | Hmmm… this isn't going to be as easy as it looks! |
| Acceptance | Maybe things can't always go the way I want. |
| Active approach | Make a list of options. |

(adapted from Padesky, 1995)

## HOW RESILIENCE HELPS YOUR SELF-ESTEEM AND EMOTIONAL STRENGTH

A combination of factors contributes to resilience. As stated earlier, it is not one individual attribute, but rather a process involving both internal cognitive (thinking) and personality factors and the functioning of external protective factors, such as caring adults. One of the primary factors in resilience is having caring and supportive relationships within and outside the family. Relationships that create love and trust, provide role models, and offer encouragement and reassurance help bolster a person's resilience.

Several additional factors are associated with resilience, including:

▶ *the capacity to make realistic plans and take steps to carry them out*
▶ *a positive view of yourself and confidence in your strengths and abilities*
▶ *skills in communication and problem solving*
▶ *the capacity to manage strong feelings and impulses.*

All of these are factors that people can develop within themselves.

### Insight
Developing resilience is a personal journey. People do not all react the same to traumatic and stressful life events. An approach to building resilience that works for one person might not work for another. People use varying strategies.

Think about what being resilient means to you, and identify the areas of your life where a more resilient outlook might be helpful to you. Your other learning about emotional intelligence is all part of developing resilience. It will fit together well and increase your emotional intelligence competencies generally.

# 10 THINGS TO REMEMBER

1   *If your resilience is good you will rebound more quickly from setbacks than those with less resilience, who dwell on their problems and may turn to unhealthy coping mechanisms.*

2   *Resilience can be a real asset in times of stress and upset.*

3   *Resilience gives you the ability to adapt more easily to difficult situations.*

4   *Learning the characteristics of resilience will help you to develop them.*

5   *If you can recover quickly from disruptive change, illness or misfortune then both your resilience and self-esteem are good.*

6   *Get connected. You will feel stronger and more confident when you create strong, positive relationships with family and friends who can listen to your concerns and offer support.*

7   *Learn from your experiences. When you come through something difficult, think about what you learned from this that was positive, and apply this learning to similar situations you face in the future.*

8   *Improve your positive self-reflection. When you have come through a difficult experience, be proud of yourself.*

9   *Focus on and recognize the three sources of resilience: 'I have'; 'I am' and 'I can'.*

10  *Develop your own strategy to improve your resilience.*

# 12

# Developing as a person to increase self-esteem

In this chapter you will learn:
- *the values that create good self-esteem*
- *how to practise your new values on a regular basis*
- *how to recover from the irrecoverable*
- *the skills to help you to tackle guilt and shame*
- *to bring all your new skills and efforts together with an easy-to-follow goal plan.*

## The keys to the kingdom: your values

> *When you have gone so far that you can't manage one more step, then you've gone just half the distance that you're capable of.*

(Greenland proverb)

Over the years, a great deal of research has been undertaken by psychologists worldwide to pinpoint the most important values we, as human beings, need to develop in order to feel truly happy and contented. Let's look together at some of those that get flagged up again and again as making a huge difference to people's lives.

If you still suffer from a variety of negative thoughts and emotions, don't worry. These are giving you valuable information about the areas in which you can make changes. If you feel gloomy and sad, then you need to focus on developing the value of *cheerfulness*. If life seems flat and dreary, then you can learn to build *passion* into your life. If you feel inadequate and unable to achieve your goals, then some *determination* will make a difference.

## POSITIVE CHANGES: MAKING A CONTRIBUTION

If you can consistently develop the idea of contributing to others' well-being, the sense of pride and self-esteem you will feel will be more than any accumulation of wealth, celebrity or accomplishment can ever give.

Positive psychologist, Professor Martin Seligman (2003) gave a class of students an assignment that involved doing one altruistic act and one pleasurable act every day for a week. He asked them to rate the 'feel good' factor that they got from these things. He discovered that while initially the 'feel good' factor for both pleasurable and altruistic acts was similar, over the following week, when the exercise was over, the 'feel good' factor for the altruistic acts remained far higher than that for the pleasurable acts.

Not only does altruism raise your self-esteem (and rightly so), but the positive feelings will stay with you, rather than fade away.

## Exercise

Undertake Martin Seligman's experiment.

▶ *In a small way, either at work or at home, for one week ensure that you do one pleasurable act and one altruistic act daily.*
▶ *Rate the 'feel good' factor for each act from 1 to 10 (where 1 = okay and 10 = very high). Note down your ratings and a week later revisit them.*
▶ *Re-rate the 'feel good' factor for each act.*

Which acts still give you the highest rating?

---

## Which values are important to you?

> *One of the most difficult things to give away is kindness, for it is usually returned.*
>
> Mark Ortman

Which are the values that guide your life? Are there values that you wish you had, but don't feel that you possess? If not, why not? Write a list of the core values that are meaningful to you, and which you consider would enhance your self-esteem.

Your self-esteem will grow considerably if you decide which values and attributes are important to you and then make a real effort to develop them and to incorporate them into your life. However if you don't quite achieve them, still remember to accept yourself. Let's look at some of the attributes that can make a real and positive contribution to your self-esteem.

## Determination

This is an attribute that you must possess or develop if you are going to create lasting self-esteem for yourself. Determination is the quality that will help you to meet challenges and overcome setbacks. It is what will make the difference between feeling totally stuck, and moving forwards powerfully and confidently.

## Love and warmth

You can develop these qualities by using many of the skills you have already worked on – most importantly, focusing on others rather than yourself. Stop seeing everything as being about you; become genuinely interested in and caring of other people and their problems and situations. Ask yourself what you could do to help, even if it is nothing more than listening, or being available. Don't always respond to anger with anger – see if you can melt anger by responding with warmth and compassion. This isn't weakness, it is strength (and quite hard to do).

## Appreciation and gratitude

Take a moment to stop thinking about what you want that you don't have and then think about what you do have. Concentrate on appreciating all the good things that have come into your life, the helpful things that people have done for you and the joy of what you have achieved. You will enhance your life greatly by thinking in this more appreciative way.

## Insight

A good way of deciding which values you consider important is to pick someone whom you admire for their character (rather than their skills or abilities) and write down which qualities you consider they possess that make them an admirable person.

## Forgiveness

When you fail to forgive someone, you are the one who is left feeling disturbed and upset. Taking a 'Why should I...?' or 'How could they...?' approach is all very well, but you are the one who will remain resentful and bitter. How does this help you? Forgiveness is what allows us to move on. It creates respect from others and gives us self-respect. It is worth working on.

## Humour and cheerfulness

These are very visible qualities and necessary ones. Being happy within yourself but not sharing this happiness with others is only half of a good thing. Being overtly cheerful will make the people around you happier as well. Think of it this way. When things are tough, does not being cheerful make things any better?

## Humility and integrity

See yourself as neither inferior nor superior to anyone else. Treat others in this same way. Have respect for the simple person; don't be in awe of the powerful person. Use your best endeavours at all times without looking for praise or reward.

## Excitement, passion and vitality

These are qualities you can actually bring into your life quite quietly. They don't have to involve being a noisy extrovert, bubbling with ideas (although they can) but rather they encourage you to think proactively and get moving! You cannot be excited and passionate if you are slumped in a chair listening to your personal fault finder running you down.

## Flexibility

Flexibility as a value? Yes, it is one that will almost guarantee feeling good. Consider the thinking skills you have learned. These could also be called 'learning to think flexibly'. Or: 'if your approach isn't working, change your approach.' Being flexible is about being willing to change your rules for living, your assumptions, the personal meaning you attach to things and your actions. Throughout your life there will be aspects you are unable to control, so adopting a flexible approach to the meaning of these items will enable you to still accept yourself.

## Insight

Learn to focus much more on developing basic qualities, rather than despairing over your weaknesses. If you do this, your weaknesses may disappear, or you may view them in a less critical light.

## Creating your personal plan

We hope that you now have an idea of the personal values that you would like to improve or possess. Within the scope of this book we are not able to work in detail with you on each one of these values, but we can help you to develop a plan that you can work on yourself on an ongoing basis.

We also suggest that you consider reading in further depth about these values. You could read:

▶ *The Art of Happiness* by His Holiness the Dalai Lama
▶ *Authentic Happiness* by Martin Seligman
▶ *The Seven Habits of Highly Successful People* by Steven Covey.

Each of these books discusses in depth the acquisition of the basic core values that have been identified throughout history – across nationhood and different religious beliefs – to be those that will bring us lasting happiness.

## Exercise

Now start work on developing your personal plan for developing values, using the one we give you opposite, or by devising one of your own to suit your needs. You can build on it over days, weeks and months in order to enhance your own core values, and/or help you to master new ones.

▶ First, fill in the overview. This will help to clarify where you are now, and what you need to work on.
▶ After four weeks of work, you can re-evaluate what improvements you have made and assess what you need to do further.

## Working on your values

Once you have filled in the developing values personal plan overview, use the following log on a weekly basis for four weeks.

**Developing values: my personal plan**

---

**Overview**
Value(s) that I would like to develop/develop further:


Elements of these values that I possess now:
(Rate how strongly you feel you possess each value at present as
a percentage, where 0% = not at all and 100% = totally)


After four weeks
How have my present values improved, and what new values do
I now possess?
(Rate them now. Has your rating improved?)


What further work to do I need to do?
(For example, do you need to record how you are doing for a
further four weeks? Are there certain opportunities you are not
taking? Do you care more about some values than others?)

---

## Exercise

Make a start on your weekly log. Use the one we give you
here or devise your own.

▶ *Work on one new value at a time. In Week 2 you can
introduce a second value, while continuing with the first,
and in Week 3, a third value, and so on. You will need*
*(Contd)*

to focus on ensuring that you do achieve these values, even if this means that you must make extra effort as you introduce new behaviours and ways of being that will reflect them.

▶ After four weeks, you may find that the values are beginning to become second nature. If you are still struggling, continue with the written exercise for a further four weeks – or as long as it takes for you to feel that they are a more natural part of you.

▶ You are free to make changes as you go along. You will only be able to measure your improved 'feel good' factor as you act out new behaviours. Some may surprise you, for example: you might start doing more for others reluctantly, only to discover that your feel good rating is much higher than you had predicted. Equally, you may set great store by being flexible, only to find that, unless you are careful, you are simply 'giving in' to things too easily. Redefine your values in the light of what you discover as you work on them.

Decide where you will keep the log so that it is easy to find when you need to make any notes in it. Promise yourself that you will keep this log on a regular basis for at least one month.

## Developing values: my weekly log

Week 1 (date)

Value 1                          Present rating

I have used this value … times

List the occasions


Improved rating for value 1

**Week 2** (date)

Value 1                                          Present rating

Value 2                                          Present rating

I have used these values ... times

List the occasions


Improved rating for values 1 and 2

**Week 3** (date)

Value 1                                          Present rating

Value 2                                          Present rating

Value 3                                          Present rating

I have used these values ... times

List the occasions


Improved rating for values 1, 2 and 3

*(Contd)*

**Week 4** (date)

Value 1                                    Present rating

Value 2                                    Present rating

Value 3                                    Present rating

Value 4                                    Present rating

I have used these values ... times

List the occasions

Improved rating for values 1, 2, 3 and 4

## Tackling serious errors of judgement

Low self-esteem is not always simply an error of thinking. It can sometimes be caused by a serious error of judgement.

Sometimes in our lives we make mistakes that have serious consequences and are hard to live with, and the resulting guilt and shame can leave us not knowing how to recover.

But we can. If we behaved in a bad or stupid way in the past, this does not mean that we are a bad or stupid person through and through. It is simply more evidence that you are fallible. We can learn from such experiences and perhaps become even better people in the future in our desire to actively change our lives.

## Peter's story

Peter worked at an ambulance call centre, responsible for answering incoming calls and prioritizing them, so that ambulances were always immediately on the scene for the most serious incidents first.

One day, Peter received two calls at the same time that seemed equally serious. However, he only had one ambulance immediately available and he had to make a decision as to where to send it. Soon after he made his decision, Peter felt that it had perhaps been the wrong one and became quite traumatized by this thought. He ruminated on whether someone had not received best care because of the choice he had been forced to make. Following this incident, Peter found it harder and harder to continue with the job, and eventually handed in his notice.

Peter kept wondering whether he had made other decisions that had been wrong. His sense of guilt at what he might have done would not leave him and he found it hard to feel good about himself again.

Then a friend, concerned for Peter's welfare, made the suggestion that – while Peter could not undo the past – he could use his experience to help others in the future. As a result, Peter joined the Samaritans and started helping those who felt they had made poor decisions in their lives they were finding hard to live. This enabled him to make a real contribution to the lives of others. It also helped him to realize that we all make (or believe we may have made) bad decisions sometimes, but that does not mean we are not people of integrity and value.

## Exercise

Complete this exercise *only if* this cause of low self-esteem applies to you.

▶ *If you believe you are worthless and feel depressed due to past transgressions, painful though this will be, revisit them now and write them down if you can. Keep them by you as you read on, where you will learn the skills to deal with them. (If you think this exercise will be overwhelming emotionally, of course you don't have to do it. It is your choice.)*

▶ *Three important questions which will help you to move forward when bad events happen for which you feel you were to blame, are:*
  ▷ *'What can I learn from this?'*
  ▷ *'In what way am I stronger as a result of this experience?'*
  ▷ *'What can I actively do to make some positive contribution, based on my experience?'*

There are many examples of people who recover their self-esteem by acknowledging and accepting what they have done as a human failing, forgiving themselves, and then using that knowledge to become stronger and possibly actively help others.

## POSITIVE ACTIVITY

Think of the number of reformed drug addicts who lecture in schools and colleges, telling their own stories and attempting to inspire young people to better lives; people who have misused alcohol and lecture on the evils of drink – even murderers who go on to reform and live useful lives. Ask yourself: 'If I cannot put this right, how can I at least create some good from it?' This might simply involve being open with others about past behaviour – and the consequences of it for you – so they have an opportunity to learn not to take the same path.

### FORGIVENESS

Self-forgiveness is just as important as forgiving others. You need to work on both of these aspects of forgiveness together. How can you forgive yourself if you cannot forgive others? Equally, as you learn to forgive others, why can you not learn to forgive yourself as well?

### SELF-ACCEPTANCE

Self-acceptance is so powerful because it does not rely on being perfect in order to feel good about oneself. Be kind to yourself and strive to do better, to move forward positively – but accept your past imperfections as being normal human frailty, rather than rendering you a terrible human being. It also means being honest with others about yourself – if you are ashamed to talk about your fallibilities, how can you learn to accept them? You will probably find that in opening up to others, that they will not judge nearly as harshly as you judge yourself – you will learn to view your behaviour in a less damning light.

## Insight

Don't dwell on your past misdemeanours and allow your personal fault finder to hound you. Use positive activity, forgiveness and self-acceptance as skills to create or restore your self-esteem.

# Deeply held negative feelings

In spite of your good efforts, we appreciate that for some of you, you really believe that you are worthless, useless or a failure as a person and these ideas are so deeply held that nothing you do will seem to shift them.

We discussed early on in the book how low self-esteem can come from childhood experiences, and where these have been especially traumatic, this is very deep-seated. You are used to being strongly judgemental of yourself – and this can overspill into being strongly judgemental of others as well. How do you overcome this?

In the same way that a person who misuses alcohol may need to stop drinking totally, your own way forward is to stop judging – totally. You must learn to stop evaluating both yourself and others as being good or bad, indifferent, right or wrong.

This will require a great deal of willpower and commitment, but the rewards can be enormous. As you stop judging others, you will learn to stop judging yourself. You will come to learn that we cannot quantify good or bad, right or wrong. Our views are often subjective, and learning acceptance of them will be quite empowering. Here are some examples of what you can do:

▶ *You can give up moral judgements on the behaviour of others. This can be hard – especially in some circumstances – but you can start saying to yourself that they are making what they consider to be their best choice of behaviour available, according to their own needs and values at the time.*
▶ *When you read newspapers or watch television news programmes, stop yourself from automatically making an instant 'right or wrong' judgement.*
▶ *Stop rating both yourself and others as being better or worse than anyone else. Simply accept people as unique individuals.*
▶ *Stop using critical descriptions, such as 'selfish', 'stupid', 'ugly', 'lazy' and so on.*

- *Stop blaming anyone else for your own negative feelings and unhappiness.*
- *Stop judging yourself in any way. This includes your thoughts, your traits and your behaviours. Accept yourself as a fallible human being.*

### Insight

If you work on not judging others, you will be much kinder to yourself. This is a hard skill to learn but we know its huge value in challenging deeply held beliefs of worthlessness. Just do it.

### Exercise

- *On a weekly and ongoing basis, select one person you know whom you don't especially like.*
- *Consider the specific aspects that you dislike about them (write them down if you need to).*
- *Now spend some time either rewriting them, or going over them in your mind in a non-judgemental way.*
- *If you have contact with this person, practise being pleasant and non-judgemental towards them.*

Most importantly, be aware of how they treat you in return and how you feel afterwards.

## Feedback from others can be helpful

Total reliance on feedback from others is self-defeating, since it means that if we are not getting praise and rewards to back up our own thinking, we lose confidence and retreat to the world of low self-esteem. However, this is not to say we should discount it altogether.

'Other esteem' can be a valuable and helpful ally for several reasons:

▶ *It assists you to keep track of how you are doing.*
▶ *It is an aide, a scorecard. It is input that tallies with our output. It helps us survive low periods when we find it hard to get self-motivated. Someone else paying us a compliment, giving us congratulations, even simply smiling and being friendly, can have a very positive 'lifting' effect.*
▶ *It makes you challenge your personal fault finder.*

A further reason that 'other esteem' is extremely helpful is when our own view of ourselves is distorted. We tend to re-evaluate our opinions of ourselves when someone makes a comment that goes against our own thinking. For example: if you are berating yourself for being selfish and thoughtless but a friend comments to you that they always find you to be very kind and thoughtful, it makes you rethink your own position; it helps you to discover your hidden qualities.

Lastly, 'other esteem' is helpful in offering us insights into positive qualities we possess that we may have been unaware of:

▶ *'You always look so nice when you smile.'*
▶ *'You may not realize it but your patience has made a real difference to me.'*
▶ *'How deft you are to do that so quickly.'*

Qualities you had no idea about get pointed out to you and again help you to reassess your view of yourself in a more positive light.

## Insight
You do not have to depend on input from others for your self-esteem, but accept it as a very helpful tool to keep your own perspective realistic rather than negative, and to learn to discover qualities that you may not have even known about.

## Exercise

How often in the past week (or longer, if necessary) have you had input from anyone else that has been at odds with your worst view of yourself? It can be as simple as the post person smiling at you, or the neighbour waving.

▶ *What negative view might this challenge? For example, your view that you are unlikable? Or that you are not very approachable?*
▶ *Write as many instances down as you can think of.*

This is a good exercise to do on a regular (weekly) basis.

### DISCOVERING HIDDEN QUALITIES

As you have just learned, 'other esteem' helps us to discover positive qualities about ourselves that we were unaware that we had.

Glenn Shiraldi (2003) describes an exercise you can do with your friends to help each of you discover more about your positive qualities. You can do this with just one or two people, but the more the merrier.

## Exercise

▶ *Gather everyone round and give each person a pen and sheet of paper. Write your own name at the top, and then pass the sheet to the person on your right. Each person then writes three points that he/she admires or appreciates about the person named on the sheet of paper, before passing it on to the next person, who does the same. Shiraldi suggests that you scatter your*

*(Contd)*

comments around the sheet, so that it is hard to identify who wrote what.

▶ *Once the lists have been completed by everyone, they are read aloud – your comments being read out by the person to your left, and so on.*

▶ *When the comments are read out, don't devalue them by making deprecating remarks such as 'What are you after?' or 'Obviously no one is wearing glasses/knows what I'm really like' and so on.*

▶ *When the comments are read out, they are often different for everyone, which adds to their value and genuineness. You may not have the same qualities as your best friend, but you both have a great amount to feel positive about.*

This is an excellent activity within families – especially if you have children (who can also suffer from low self-esteem, of course). Children are usually over the moon to receive positive compliments. A real bond is created between the members of the group.

Suggest that everyone keeps their own sheet of paper. They are excellent to refer back to at times when our personal fault finder is on the march, and we could use an emotional lift.

### Insight

Accept that you have more positive qualities than you may be aware of. Many of them are only visible to others, because you either take them for granted, or don't realize how attractive you appear when you smile, or offer to help a friend.

Do plan to have a go at this exercise. You will not necessarily be able to do this immediately unless you have a houseful of people 'on tap', but set it up – either at work or at home – on the basis that it will benefit all who take part.

# Moving forward: your goal plan

A great deal of the hard work you have done so far has required you to focus on achieving a specific goal, and then doing what it takes to achieve that goal.

Now, to consistently increase your self-esteem and keep it in good shape, you need to learn to set goals regularly, as part of your life. Many of you will have heard of the SMART model for goal setting. If not, the initials stand for:

*Specific Measurable Achievable Realistic Time-limited*

As you make your goal plan, ensure that each one meets all the above criteria.

What is the most important word in a goal plan? It's ACTION. You can write as much as you like, in as much detail as you like, on as many sheets of paper as you like, but ACTION – actually doing something – is the only thing that will make a difference.

Put your goal plan on paper. Research has shown that when we write down our goals, we have a much (much) better chance of achieving them. Your goal plan should look something like this example (with much more writing space, particularly for the 'specific action' side of the plan).

| My goal(s) | Specific action I am committed to take to achieve my goal(s) |
|---|---|
| Week 1 | |
| Week 2 | |
| ...and so on... | |

- *Make your goals as specific as possible, since that is what makes them easy.*
- *Ensure that your mini-goals are achievable. We want goals that make it easy for us to feel good and hard for us to feel bad.*
- *Make sure your goals are challenging but not overwhelming. Goal setting needs to become part of your life, not something you give up very quickly because it is time consuming and leading to more failures than successes.*
- *If having high self-esteem is one of your goals, you now have the skill and knowledge base to go about it.*

## Exercise

Using the skills you have been working on in this chapter, write your own goal plan for high self-esteem. Consider using similar plans for other areas of your life. You will achieve more, in less time, and feel good for having done so.

### Insight

You can achieve whatever you wish if you know exactly and specifically what you want, you have the skills to achieve it – and you have a plan.

We wish you the richer, better and more confident life you will deserve as you achieve success through your efforts. We want you to be pleased to be *You*!

# 10 THINGS TO REMEMBER

1 *Negative thoughts can give you valuable information about areas of your life in which you can make changes that will improve your self-esteem.*

2 *Before you can develop your values, you need to consider which are the most important to you.*

3 *Make a personal plan to develop the values you have selected; this will help you to clarify where you are now and what you need to work on.*

4 *Work on one new value at a time; you will soon find that supporting and practising these values become second nature to you.*

5 *Low self-esteem can be caused by an error of judgement; self-acceptance allows us to forgive ourselves and move on.*

6 *Move forward from bad events for which you feel you are to blame by asking what you can learn from the experience.*

7 *Practise suspending judgement totally; as you stop judging others, it becomes easier to stop judging yourself.*

8 *'Other esteem' can be valuable and uplifting when you are working hard on change yourself.*

9 *'Other esteem' can help you to discover qualities that you did not recognize in yourself.*

10 *Setting goal plans keeps you structured and focused but no matter how good your plans are,* actually doing something is the only thing that will make a real difference.

# Appendix A: professional assistance

Where problems of low self-esteem are chronic and deep-seated – and where you have done your hardest to eliminate these difficulties on your own with only partial success – you might wish to consider professional assistance.

Psychological therapy can be very helpful in this regard. In this book, we have taken a cognitive behavioural and rational emotive behavioural therapy approach. If these approaches appeal to you, then you might wish to work with a qualified therapist who is accredited by either the Association for Rational Emotive Behaviour Therapy or the British Association for Behaviour and Cognitive Psychotherapies. These two professional bodies maintain an online register of accredited therapists.

Insight-based (psychodynamic) therapy will explore your past, looking for unresolved unconscious conflicts that are holding you back in the present.

Some therapy is described as 'integrative', where the therapist will draw on different orientations to suit the client and/or the problem at different points in the therapy.

Life coaching can also be useful where you feel stuck in a rut, as it is a very goal-orientated and motivational approach.

The following websites provide access to some of the organizations and registers you might wish to contact to find a therapist who can help you. Be sure to check that the therapist is professionally accredited to the organization you contact.

Association for Rational Emotive Behaviour Therapy
www.arebt.org

British Association for Counselling and Psychotherapy
www.bacp.co.uk

British Association for Behavioural and Cognitive Psychotherapies
www.babcp.org.uk

CBT Register UK
www.cbtregisteruk.com

UK Council for Psychotherapy
www.ukcp.org.uk

Association for Coaching
www.associationforcoaching.com

Centre for Coaching
www.centreforcoaching.com

Centre for Stress Management
www.managingstress.com

American Counseling Association
www.counseling.org

American Psychological Association
www.apa.org

Association for Professional Executive Coaching and Supervision
www.apecs.org

Australian Psychological Society
www.psychology.org.au

British Psychological Society
www.bps.org.uk

European Mentoring & Coaching Council
www.emccouncil.org

International Coach Federation
www.coachfederation.org.uk

National Board of Certified Counselors (USA)
www.nbcc.org

Society for Coaching Psychology
www.societyforcoachingpsychology.net

# Appendix B: alcohol dependency and abusive relationships

The following two areas of low self-esteem can be complex problems. As such, they are beyond the remit of this book to deal with in depth, but we wish to highlight them and the resources available to anyone who is struggling with these issues.

---

## Low self-esteem and alcohol

For many of us, a drink or two to calm our nerves before a difficult meeting, a daunting social situation or simply to relax can be beneficial. However, using it as a prop to disguise the real problem – lack of confidence and low self-esteem – can cause people to become alcohol dependent. You may begin to make the erroneous connection that you can *only* cope if you have a drink.

We need to stress that you need to be honest with yourself about any alcohol dependency. While we hope that improving your self-esteem may reduce your reliance on alcohol, alcohol is addictive. You may find it too difficult to stop on your own.

If you want to reduce your alcohol intake, but would like some help to do so, we would suggest that you read one of the following books or contact AA. Do not wait until you have a really serious problem to do this. Nip it in the bud.

### BOOKS

Bert Pluymen, *The Thinking Person's Guide to Sobriety* (Griffin, 2006)

(If you are dithering over the 'Do I have a problem' question, this book will help you decide.)

Alan Carr, *Alan Carr's Easy Way to Control Alcohol* (Arcturus Foulsham, 2002)

### WEBSITES

www.alcoholics-anonymous.org.uk
Alcoholics Anonymous office website.

www.smartrecovery.co.uk
Smart Recovery UK, based on the rational emotive behavioural approach to any addiction.

www.aamolly.org.uk
For more informal information, this is an unofficial website full of helpful ideas as well as opportunities to chat through forums.

---

## Low self-esteem and abusive relationships

Many people stay in relationships that are both verbally abusive and physically violent because their self-esteem is so low that they lack the confidence to leave. These destructive relationships can range from occasional outbursts to regular violence. If you are in an abusive relationship and wonder if you should leave – or know you should, but lack the confidence to do so – you can seek help and we suggest some resources below.

### BOOKS

Mia Kirshenbaum, *Too Good to Leave, Too Bad to Stay: A Step-by-Step Guide to Help You Decide Whether to Stay in or Get Out of Your Relationship* (Michael Joseph, 1997)

Patricia Evans, *The Verbally Abusive Relationship: How to Recognize it and How to Respond* (Adams Media Corporation, 2002)

Dawn Bradley Perry, *The Domestic Violence Sourcebook* (McGraw Hill Contemporary, 2000)

### WEBSITE

www.bbc.co.uk/relationships/domesticviolence
Total support – from deciding whether you are really in an abusive relationship to where to go to get help.

# Taking it further

We hope you have enjoyed reading this book and have benefited from the challenging activities. If you wish to contact either of the authors directly, their details are as follows:

Professor Stephen Palmer PhD
Centre for Coaching
156 Westcombe Hill
London
SE3 7DH
palmer@centresofexpertise.com

Christine Wilding CMCIPD
Briarwood House
Talisman Way
Epsom
Surrey
KT17 3PQ
chrissyw2@aol.com

# References and further reading

Dr Robert Anthony, *How to Raise your Self-Esteem* (Random House, 1997)

Nathaniel Branden, *Six Pillars of Self-Esteem* (Bantam, 1995)

Meredith Bunch, *Creating Confidence* (Kogan Page,1999)

David Burns, *10 Days to Great Self-Esteem* (Vermilion, 1993)

David Burns, *The Feeling Good Handbook* (Plume, 1999)

Jack Canfield, Mark Hansen & Les Hewitt, *The Power of Focus* (Vermilion, 2000)

Alan Carr, *Positive Psychology* (Routledge, 2004)

Thomas Cash, *The Body Image Workbook* (New Harbinger, 2008)

Cary Cooper & Stephen Palmer, *Conquer your Stress* (Chartered Institute of Personal Development, 2000)

Stephen Covey, *The Seven Habits of Highly Successful People* (Simon & Schuster, 1989)

HH The Dalai Lama, *The Art of Happiness* (Hodder & Stoughton, 1998)

Philippa Davies, *Increasing Confidence* (Dorling Kindersley, 2003)

Melanie Fennell, *Overcoming Low Self-Esteem* (Basic Books, 2009)

Darrell Franken, *Personal Strengths* (Wellness Publications, 2006)

Shakti Gawain, *Creative Visualization* (New World Library, 2002)

Terry Gillen, *Assertiveness* (Chartered Institute of Personal Development, 1997)

Paul Hauck, *How to Be Your Own Best Friend* (Sheldon Press, 1998)

Tim Laurence, *You Can Change Your Life* (Hodder Mobius, 2004)

Matthew McKay & Patrick Fanning, *Self-Esteem* (New Harbinger, 2000)

Christine Padesky & Dennis Greenberger, *Mind Over Mood* (Guilford, 1995)

Stephen Palmer, 'Self-acceptance: concept, techniques and interventions' in *The Rational Emotive Behaviour Therapist* (5, 1, 3–30; 1997)

Stephen Palmer, Cary Cooper & Kate Thomas, *Creating a Balance: Managing Stress* (British Library, 2003)

Stephen Palmer & Christine Wilding, *Moody to Mellow* (Hodder Arnold, 2005)

Stephen Palmer & Cary Cooper, *How to Deal with Stress* (Kogan Page, 2010)

Martin Perry, *Confidence Booster Workout* (Hamlyn, 2003)

Anthony Robbins, *Awaken The Giant Within* (Pocket Books, 2001)

Glenn Schiraldi, *The Self-Esteem Workbook* (New Harbinger, 2003)

Martin Seligman, *Authentic Happiness* (Nicholas Brealey, 2003)

Martin Seligman, *Learned Optimism* (Simon & Schuster, 1998)

Christine Webber, *Get the Self-Esteem Habit* (Hodder & Stoughton, 2002)

Christine Wilding, *Teach Yourself Emotional Intelligence* (Hodder Education, 2007)

Christine Wilding & Stephen Palmer, *Zero to Hero: From Cringing to Confident in 100 Steps* (Hodder Arnold, 2006)

Jeffrey Young, *Reinventing Your Life* (Penguin Putnam Inc USA, 1993)

# Index

# Image credits